¡Ven conmigo!

Holt Spanish
Level 1

Chapter Teaching Resources
Book 2

HOLT, RINEHART AND WINSTON
Harcourt Brace & Company
Austin • New York • Orlando • Atlanta • San Francisco • Boston • Dallas • Toronto • London

Contributing Writers:

Rosann Batteiger
Mary Diehl
Diane Donaho
Carol Ann Marshall
Jean Miller
Amy Propps
Dana Todd

Some material appears in this book from other HRW publications.

Printed in the United States of America

ISBN 0-03-094961-0

2 3 4 5 6 7 8 9 021 99 98 97 96 95

Contents

CAPÍTULO 8

¡A comer!

To the Teacher

For your convenience, most of the ancillary material available for use with Level 1 of the **¡Ven conmigo!** Spanish program is packaged together, by chapter, in three *Chapter Teaching Resources* books. Each book contains the material for four chapters.

Chapter Teaching Resources, Book 1 Chapters 1-4
Chapter Teaching Resources, Book 2 Chapters 5-8
Chapter Teaching Resources, Book 3 Chapters 9-12

These books are designed to help you accommodate the diverse learning styles of your students.

Chapter Teaching Resources, Book 2

Each chapter contains the following instructional materials.

- **Communicative Activities** In each chapter there are two communicative, pair-work activities that encourage students to express themselves in Spanish in realistic conversation. The activities provide language practice and also foster cooperative learning. Pair work allows students to take risks with language in a relaxed, uninhibiting, and enjoyable setting. You might want to use the first Communicative Activity after the second **paso** and the second activity after the third **paso.**
- **Teaching Transparency Masters** Accompanying the blackline masters of the *Teaching Transparencies* are suggestions for using the transparencies in the classroom. Three transparencies per chapter depict situations closely related to the three **pasos** in each chapter. The transparencies are a valuable resource for developing language skills and creating cultural awareness and understanding. You might ask students to describe what they see or to play the roles of the people in the transparencies and converse accordingly. Used in this manner, the transparencies involve students in interactive communication. You may wish to use the transparencies in your presentation of each **paso** or to re-enter and review previously learned material. The blackline masters enable you to place a copy of the transparency in the hands of each student for use in cooperative learning groups, for individual or group writing assignments, and for homework. Blackline masters of the *Map Transparencies* can be found in the transparency package, along with suggestions for using the map transparencies.
- **Additional Listening Activities** Six activities per chapter, two for each **paso** in the chapter, provide additional listening comprehension practice. Although these activities focus on the functions, vocabulary, and structures of the chapter, the content is not solely restricted to material students have already learned. To develop listening skills, students hear conversations, announcements, advertisements, radio broadcasts, phone messages, and so on, that simulate real-life listening situations and contain some unfamiliar material. Forms are provided on which students can write their responses, and the scripts of the recordings are provided for your convenience. The listening activities are recorded on the *Additional Listening Activities Audiocassettes* and on the *Audio Compact Discs*.
- **Realia** For each chapter there are two reproducible pieces of realia related to the chapter theme. This collection of material reflects life and culture in Spanish-speaking countries. Finding they can read and understand documents intended for native speakers, students experience a feeling of accomplishment that encourages them to continue learning. Together with the blackline masters of the realia, you will find suggestions for using each document in the classroom to develop listening, speaking, reading, and writing skills.
- **Situation Cards** For each **paso** of the chapter, three sets of interview questions and three situations for role-playing are provided in blackline master form. These cards are designed to stimulate conversation in the classroom. You might conduct the interviews with individual students or have students pair off and interview each other. After partners have conversed in a role-playing situation, you may want to have them change roles. To avoid having to copy the cards repeatedly, consider mounting them on cardboard and laminating them.
- **Student Response Forms** Blackline masters provide answer forms for the listening activities in the *Pupil's Edition.*
- **Quizzes** Three quizzes accompany each chapter, one quiz for each **paso.** The quizzes, which focus on the material of the **paso,** assess listening, reading, and writing skills, as well as culture. The quizzes are short enough to be administered within a class period, leaving ample time for other activities. The listening section of each quiz re-enters one of the textbook listening scripts. Reading material, in various formats, assesses comprehension of the material of each **paso.** The writing portion of each quiz asks students to

express themselves in real situations rather than fill in blanks with discrete items. The listening sections of the quizzes are recorded on the *Assessment Items Audiocassettes* and on the *Audio Compact Discs.*

- **Chapter Tests** The Chapter Tests for Chapters 1-12 include listening, reading, writing, and culture segments. They are designed to be completed in a class period. Convenient score sheets are provided with the tests. With the exception of the writing and some culture segments, the Chapter Tests are designed to facilitate mechanical or electronic scoring. You will find the listening segments for the Chapter Tests recorded on the *Assessment Items Audiocassettes* and on the *Audio Compact Discs.* See the *Assessment Guide* for the Mid-term Exam, the Final Exam, and Speaking Tests.
- **Scripts and Answers** Scripts for the Additional Listening Activities, the Quizzes, and the Chapter Test are found in this section. Also included are the answers to the Additional Listening Activities, the Quizzes, and the Chapter Test.
- **Answer Key for** *Practice and Activity Book* Full-size pages of the *Practice and Activity Book* for each chapter, including the preliminary chapter, have been reproduced with answers in place.

Additional Ancillaries

The following ancillaries have been packaged separately from the *Chapter Teaching Resources Books.*

- The *Assessment Guide* provides a variety of materials to help you implement portfolio assessment in your classroom, if you so choose. These materials include an explanation of portfolio assessment, as well as suggestions for setting up portfolios and selecting materials for them. Portfolio activities—oral and written—are suggested for each chapter in the textbook along with criteria for evaluating the activities. Portfolio checklists and evaluation forms are provided for both the student and the teacher. Speaking Tests for Chapters 1-12, the Mid-term Exam, and the Final Exam are also included in the *Assessment Guide.*
- The *Video Guide* provides material for both you and your students. The booklet contains all the scripts of the **¡Ven conmigo!** *Video Program and Expanded Video Program.* Blackline masters provide students with supplementary vocabulary and activities. Also, you will find background information and suggestions for additional pre-viewing, viewing, and post-viewing activities.
- The *Audiocassette Program* includes all recorded material for use with **¡Ven conmigo!** Material from each chapter of the *Pupil's Edition* is recorded on six *Textbook Audiocassettes.* The **De antemano** episode is recorded twice, once for listening and again with pauses for student repetition. Also recorded are the interviews in the **Panorama Cultural** and the listening and pronunciation activities. Two *Assessment Items Audiocassettes* provide recordings of the listening sections of the Chapter Quizzes, the Chapter Tests, the Mid-term Exam, and the Final Exam. Two *Additional Listening Activities Audiocassettes* contain the recorded scripts for the Additional Listening Activities. One *Songs Audiocassette* presents songs to be enjoyed with each chapter.
- The *Audio Compact Discs* contain all the material available on the *Audiocassette Program*, regrouped to take advantage of the easy access provided by compact disc technology. Each disc contains all the material necessary for an entire chapter: textbook activities, assessment items, additional listening activities, and songs or poems.
- The *Test Generator* software program enables you to construct your own tests to meet the needs of your own students. You can select from an array of speaking, listening, reading, writing, vocabulary, grammar, and culture items. The *Test Generator* can also serve as a valuable source of additional activities to practice the chapter material. The *Test Generator* is available in the Macintosh® version or the IBM® and Compatibles version.
- The *Videodisc Program and Guide* consists of six videodiscs and an accompanying guide. The discs include the entire content of the *Video Program* and the *Expanded Video Program* in this easily accessible format. The guide contains all the material in the *Video Guide* with added activities and barcodes.
- The *Practice and Activity Book, Pupil's Edition* contains contextualized vocabulary, grammar, and communication activities that are closely coordinated with the chapters of the textbook. Each chapter of the *Practice and Activity Book* provides activities for the **De antemano** and each of the three **pasos,** reading practice to supplement the **Vamos a leer** section, and cultural awareness activities that require students to apply their knowledge of Spanish-speaking cultures gleaned from the **Panorama cultural** and **Encuentro cultural** features and the **Notas culturales.** The activities, ranging from simple to complex, from controlled to open-ended, provide additional opportunities for students to develop communication skills and cultural understanding. Answers to the *Practice and Activity Book* activities are included by chapter in the *Chapter Teaching Resources Books.*

CAPÍTULO 5

El ritmo de la vida

RESOURCES

El ritmo de la vida

Chapter Teaching Resources Correlation Chart

RESOURCES	Print	Audiovisual
De antemano	*Practice and Activity Book*, p. 49	
	Video Guide OR *Videodisc Guide*	*Textbook Audiocassette 3A/Audio CD 5* *Video Program* OR *Expanded Video Program, Videocassette 2* OR *Videodisc Program, Videodisc 3A*
Primer paso	*Chapter Teaching Resources, Book 2*	
	• Teaching Transparency Master 5-1, p. 7	*Teaching Transparency 5-1*
	• Additional Listening Activities 5-1, 5-2, p. 11 —Scripts, p. 38; Answers, p. 40	*Additional Listening Activities, Audiocassette 9B/Audio CD 5*
	• Realia 5-1, p. 15, 17	
	• Situation Cards 5-1, pp. 18–19	
	• Student Response Forms, p. 20	
	• Quiz 5-1, pp. 23–24 —Scripts, p. 41; Answers, p. 42	*Assessment Items, Audiocassette 7B/Audio CD 5*
	Practice and Activity Book, pp. 50–52 —Answers: *Chapter Teaching Resources, Book 2*, pp. 46–48	
	Native Speaker Activity Book, pp. 21–25 —Answers: *Chapter Teaching Resources, Book 2*, pp. 57–58	
	Videodisc Guide	*Videodisc Program, Videodisc 3A*
	Video Guide	*Video Program* OR *Expanded Video Program, Videocassette 2*
Segundo paso	*Chapter Teaching Resources, Book 2*	
	• Communicative Activity 5-1, pp. 3–4	
	• Teaching Transparency Master 5-2, p. 8	*Teaching Transparency 5-2*
	• Additional Listening Activities 5-3, 5-4, p. 12 —Scripts, pp. 38–39; Answers, p. 40	*Additional Listening Activities, Audiocassette 9B/Audio CD 5*
	• Realia 5-2, pp. 16, 17	
	• Situation Cards 5-2, pp. 18–19	
	• Student Response Forms, p. 22	
	• Quiz 5-2, pp. 25–26 —Scripts, p. 41; Answers, p. 42	*Assessment Items, Audiocassette 7B/Audio CD 5*
	Practice and Activity Book, pp. 53–55 —Answers: *Chapter Teaching Resources, Book 2*, pp. 49–51	
	Native Speaker Activity Book, pp. 21–25 —Answers: *Chapter Teaching Resources, Book 2*, pp. 57–58	
	Videodisc Guide	*Videodisc Program, Videodisc 3A*
Tercer paso	*Chapter Teaching Resources, Book 2*	
	• Communicative Activity 5-2, pp. 5–6	
	• Teaching Transparency Master 5-3, p. 9	*Teaching Transparency 5-3*
	• Additional Listening Activities 5-5, 5-6, p. 13 —Scripts, pp. 38–39; Answers, p. 40	*Additional Listening Activities, Audiocassette 9B/Audio CD 5*
	• Realia 5-2, pp. 16, 17	
	• Situation Cards 5-3, pp. 18–19	
	• Student Response Forms, p. 22	
	• Quiz 5-3, pp. 27–28 —Scripts, p. 41; Answers, p. 42	*Assessment Items, Audiocassette 7B/Audio CD 5*
	Practice and Activity Book, pp. 56–58 —Answers: *Chapter Teaching Resources, Book 2*, pp. 52–54	
	Native Speaker Activity Book, pp. 21–25 —Answers: *Chapter Teaching Resources, Book 2*, pp. 57–58	
	Videodisc Guide	*Videodisc Program, Videodisc 3A*

ASSESSMENT

Paso Quizzes
- *Chapter Teaching Resources, Book 2*
  Quizzes pp. 23–28
  Scripts and answers pp. 41–42
- Assessment Items, *Audiocassette 7B/Audio CD 5*

Portfolio Assessment
- *Assessment Guide*, pp. 2–13. 18

Chapter Test
- *Chapter Teaching Resources, Book 2*, pp. 29–34
  Test score sheets, pp. 35–36
  Test scripts and answers, pp. 43–44
- *Assessment Guide*, Speaking Test, p. 30
- Assessment Items, *Audiocassette 7B/Audio CD 5*

Test Generator, Chapter 5

Communicative Activity 5-1 A

1. You and your partner are both sales representatives for a company that makes fitness products. Your partner has just completed a survey of 100 high school students to find out how many have healthful habits. Get this information from your partner by asking how many students take part in the activities listed in the chart below. Fill out the chart with the numbers he or she gives you.

MODELO — ¿Con qué frecuencia beben agua o jugo?
— Cuarenta y dos estudiantes nunca beben agua o jugo. Cincuenta y ocho estudiantes beben agua o jugo todos los días.

	nunca	a veces	todos los días
asistir a una clase de ejercicios aeróbicos			
comer ensalada			
correr dos millas			
hacer ejercicio			
practicar un deporte			

2. You've just completed a survey of 100 high school students to find out how many have unhealthful habits. Help your partner out by answering his or her questions using the information you've compiled in the chart below.

	nunca	a veces	todos los días
comer hamburguesas con papas fritas	10	64	26
tomar refrescos	2	79	19
comer chocolate	5	80	15
mirar mucha televisión	11	25	64
caminar	2	10	88

Nombre ______________________ Clase ____________ Fecha ____________

CAPÍTULO 5

Communicative Activity 5-1B

1. You and your partner are both sales representatives for a company that makes fitness products. You have just completed a survey of 100 high school students to find out how many have healthful habits. Help your partner out by answering his or her questions using the information you've compiled in the chart below.

MODELO — ¿Con qué frecuencia beben agua o jugo?
— Cuarenta y dos estudiantes nunca beben agua o jugo. Cincuenta y ocho estudiantes beben agua o jugo todos los días.

	nunca	a veces	todos los días
asistir a una clase de ejercicios aeróbicos	27	43	30
comer ensalada	18	71	11
correr dos millas	63	28	9
hacer ejercicio	14	49	37
practicar un deporte	19	47	34

2. Your partner has just completed a survey of 100 high school students to find out how many have unhealthful habits. Get this information from your partner by asking how many students take part in the activities listed in the chart below. Fill out the chart with the numbers he or she gives you.

	nunca	a veces	todos los días
comer hamburguesas con papas fritas			
tomar refrescos			
comer chocolate			
mirar mucha televisión			
caminar			

Nombre ______________________ Clase ____________ Fecha ____________

Communicative Activity 5-2A

CAPÍTULO 5

1. You've just started working for a meteorological service in Seattle, Washington. Part of your job is to keep track of weather patterns in the Pacific Northwest. Your partner works for a meteorological service in Omaha, Nebraska. Your partner's job is to keep track of weather patterns in the central United States. Call your partner and ask him or her what the weather is like in the central part of the country. Fill in the chart with the information he or she gives you.

MODELO — ¿Qué tiempo hace en Salt Lake City en junio?
— Hace mucho calor. Nunca llueve.

Ciudad	**enero**	**julio**
St. Louis		
Dallas		
Denver		
Indianapolis		

2. Your partner in Omaha needs to track weather patterns in the Pacific Northwest. Using the information in the chart below, answer your partner's questions about the weather there.

Ciudad	**enero**	**julio**
Seattle		
Portland		
Butte		
San Francisco		

Nombre ______________________ Clase ____________ Fecha ____________

Communicative Activity 5-2B

1. You've just started working for a meteorological service in Omaha, Nebraska. Part of your job is to keep track of weather patterns in the central United States. Your partner works for a meteorological service in Seattle, Washington. He or she has called you up to find out about weather patterns in the central United States. Using the information in the chart below, answer your partner's questions about the weather.

MODELO — ¿Qué tiempo hace en Salt Lake City en junio?
— Hace mucho calor. Nunca llueve.

Ciudad	**enero**	**julio**
St. Louis	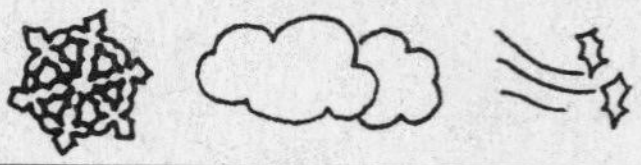	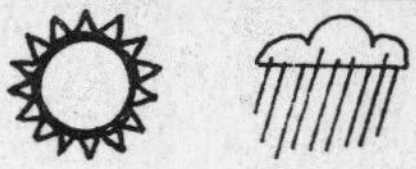
Dallas	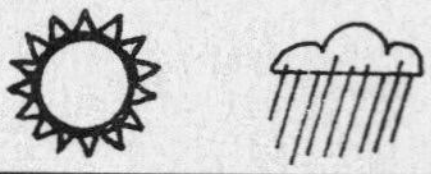	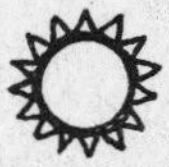
Denver	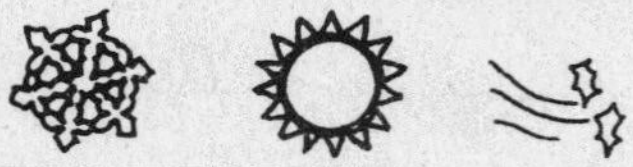	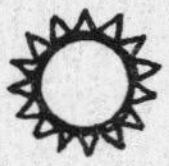
Indianapolis	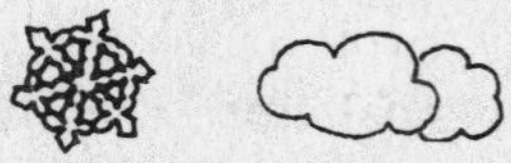	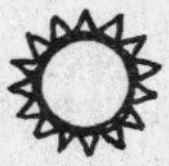

2. You now need to ask your partner in Seattle about weather patterns in the Pacific Northwest. Fill in the chart with the information he or she gives you.

Ciudad	**enero**	**julio**
Seattle		
Portland		
Butte		
San Francisco		

Nombre ______________________ Clase ____________ Fecha ____________

Teaching Transparency Master 5-1

Nombre ______________________ Clase ______________ Fecha ______________

Teaching Transparency Master 5-2

Nombre ______________________ Clase ____________ Fecha ____________

Teaching Transparency Master 5-3

Using Teaching Transparencies 5-1, 5-2, 5-3

Teaching Transparency 5-1

1. **Speaking:** Have students give names to the people pictured. Write the names on the overhead transparency. Then have students describe what each of the people is doing.
2. **Listening:** Make statements about the activities pictured. Students should respond to the statements with **cierto** or **falso**.
3. **Speaking:** Have students interview each other about which activities depicted in the transparencies they like to do during a typical week, and how often.
4. **Writing/Pair work:** Have students write five questions based on the activities depicted in the transparency. Then have students get together with a partner and answer the questions.

   MODELO **¿Quién ayuda en casa?**

Teaching Transparency 5-2

1. **Speaking:** Have students assign names to each of the people pictured in the transparency and then describe what each one is doing.
2. **Speaking:** Have students make a list of the activities depicted in the transparency and then ask each other whether or not they like to do those things. Have them report their results.
3. **Writing/Pair work:** Have students write a plan for a vacation such as the one shown in the tranparency. Then have them compare their vacation plan first with a partner, then with other students in the class.

Teaching Transparency 5-3

1. **Speaking:** Ask students what season they think it is in each illustration. Have them tell you what months they associate with the weather shown in each illustration.
2. **Listening:** Make statements about the weather or seasons in each illustration and have students say whether your statements are **cierto** or **falso**.
3. **Writing:** Have students choose a city and write a weather report for a given month or season.
4. **Writing:** Have students choose a Latin American region or city and compare the weather there to the weather where they live.
5. **Group work:** Have small groups of students prepare a "world weather" map. Each group should select a month or season, and then write a weather report for three different cities or regions during that time period.

Nombre ______________________ Clase ______________ Fecha ______________

PRIMER PASO

5-1 You will hear an interview between Ana María, an exchange student from Spain, and Roque, a reporter for the paper at Seminole High School in Miami. In the interview, Ana María talks about her life in Spain and her new lifestyle in Miami. Listen to the interview and answer the multiple-choice questions below.

1. En España, Ana María va a clases _____.
   a. cinco veces a la semana
   b. seis veces a la semana

2. Ana María dice que (*says that*) en Miami, los estudiantes _____ van a clases en coche o en autobús.
   a. nunca
   b. siempre

3. En España, Ana María _____ tiene 8 o 9 materias en el colegio.
   a. a veces
   b. siempre

4. Ana María dice que en Miami, hay un examen en una de las clases _____.
   a. todas las semanas
   b. una vez al semestre

5. En España, Ana María _____ va a un café después de clases.
   a. nunca
   b. siempre

5-2 Ana María has met a lot of people during her first few weeks at Seminole High School and she's trying to get them all straight. Listen to her conversation with Luis about some of the people she's met so far. Match up the drawings below with the names of people she and Luis discuss. Not all drawings will have a matching name.

_____ 1. Marta y Lola
_____ 2. Héctor
_____ 3. Miguel
_____ 4. Sara

a.

b.

c.

d.

e.

Additional Listening Activities

SEGUNDO PASO

5-3 Listen as Ramón talks about what he and his friends do in their free time and write their favorite activity next to their names.

1. Juan Carlos y Gabriela **asistir a conciertos**
2. Ramón ______________________
3. Sandra ______________________
4. Guillermo y Norma ______________________
5. Pedro ______________________
6. Cristina ______________________

5-4 Listen as Teresa describes a typical Saturday and number the drawings in order according to her description.

a. ______

b. ______

c. ______

d. ______

TERCER PASO

5-5 Listen to Jaime and Elena talk about some upcoming events in the next week. Fill in Elena's datebook with the events Jaime mentions. The first time you listen, write the name of each event. Then listen again and write the time it takes place in the correct space.

noviembre	
lunes 11	concierto 9:00 p.m.
martes 12	
miércoles 13	
jueves 14	
viernes 15	
sábado 16	
domingo 17	

5-6 Listen as the announcer at a Spanish-speaking radio station in Miami reads a weather report for today and match each city with the correct forecast.

_____ 1. Miami
_____ 2. San Antonio
_____ 3. Los Ángeles
_____ 4. Denver
_____ 5. Boston

a. hace sol
b. hace mucho calor
c. está lloviendo
d. hace mucho viento
e. está nevando

Additional Listening Activities

SONG

Pamplona is the capital of the region of Navarra in Spain. The **pamplonenses** celebrate their city's patron saint, San Fermín, on July 7 with a great annual fair that includes the famous **encierro de Pamplona**. For the **encierro** (*enclosure*), the authorities block several streets, and a number of bulls are let loose. Those who are daring run ahead of the bulls and try to escape them, while the crowd looks on. It is at this fair that the young people of Pamplona sing ***Uno de enero***.

Uno de enero

Uno de enero,
dos de febrero,
tres de marzo,
cuatro de abril,
cinco de mayo,
seis de junio,
siete de julio,
San Fermín.

This song is recorded on *Audio CD 5* and is also on *Audiocassette 11*: *Songs*. Although it is presented in this chapter, it can be used at any time.

Realia 5-1

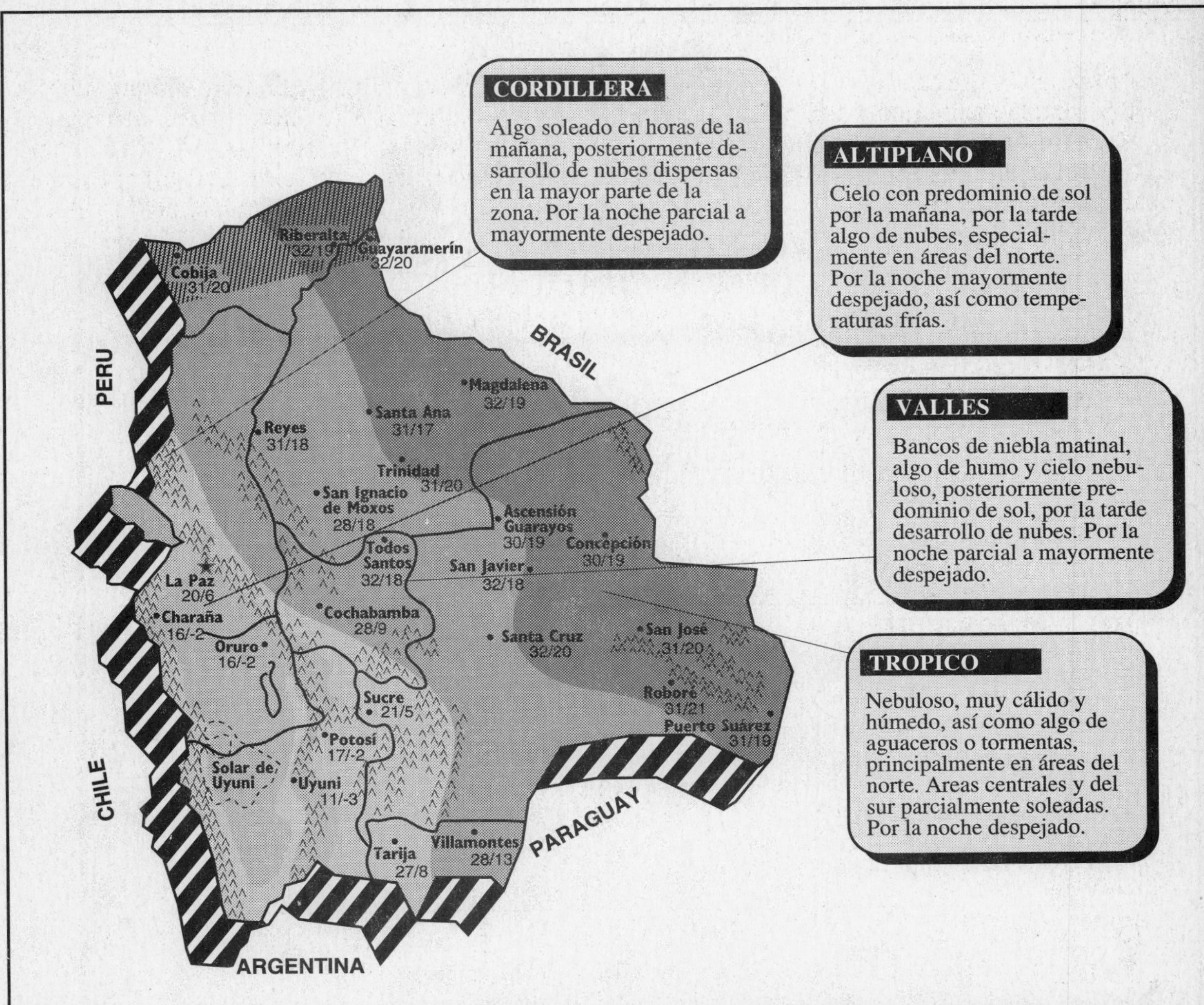
CORDILLERA
Algo soleado en horas de la mañana, posteriormente desarrollo de nubes dispersas en la mayor parte de la zona. Por la noche parcial a mayormente despejado.
ALTIPLANO
Cielo con predominio de sol por la mañana, por la tarde algo de nubes, especialmente en áreas del norte. Por la noche mayormente despejado, así como temperaturas frías.
VALLES
Bancos de niebla matinal, algo de humo y cielo nebuloso, posteriormente predominio de sol, por la tarde desarrollo de nubes. Por la noche parcial a mayormente despejado.
TROPICO
Nebuloso, muy cálido y húmedo, así como algo de aguaceros o tormentas, principalmente en áreas del norte. Areas centrales y del sur parcialmente soleadas. Por la noche despejado.
PERU
BRASIL
CHILE
PARAGUAY
ARGENTINA
Cobija 31/20
Riberalta 32/19
Guayaramerín 32/20
Magdalena 32/19
Santa Ana 31/17
Reyes 31/18
Trinidad 31/20
San Ignacio de Moxos 28/18
Ascensión Guarayos 30/19
Concepción 30/19
Todos Santos 32/18
San Javier 32/18
La Paz 20/6
Charaña 16/-2
Cochabamba 28/9
Santa Cruz 32/20
San José 31/20
Oruro 16/-2
Roboré 31/21
Puerto Suárez 31/19
Sucre 21/5
Potosí 17/-2
Solar de Uyuni
Uyuni 11/-3
Tarija 27/8
Villamontes 28/13

Nombre ______________________ Clase ____________ Fecha ____________

Realia 5-2

TEATRO MUNICIPAL
CORPORACION
CULTURAL DE LA
I. DE MUNICIPALIDAD
DE SANTIAGO

LA MUSICA, LA OPERA, LA DANZA...
PROGRAMA BALLET

	B1 19:00 hrs. Estrenos	B2 19:00 hrs.	B3 19:00 hrs.	B4 19:00 hrs.
LOS TRES MOSQUETEROS Estrenos 3 actos Música: G. Verdi, arreglos Guy Woolfenden Coreografía: André Prokovsky Escenografía y Vestuario: Peter Farmer	Martes 19 de abril	Jueves 21 de abril	Viernes 22 de abril	Sábado 23 de abril
ROMEO Y JULIETA 3 actos Música: Sergei Prokofiev Coreografía: John Cranko Escenografía y Vestuario: Elisabeth Dalton	Miércoles 15 de junio	Jueves 16 de junio	Viernes 17 de junio	Lunes 20 de junio

ESTUDIANTES (En venta a partir del 1º de diciembre)

Para los estudiantes se ha previsto abonos especiales en todas las series de concierto y ballet, en las siguientes localidades:

- **Balcón lateral**
- **Palco lateral 1er piso da fila**
- **Palco lateral 2o piso 2a fila**

Los precios de estos abonos son:

- **Conciertos:** $1.000 (10 conciertos)
- **Ballet:** $1.000 (6 ballets)
- Al entrar a los espectáculos, los estudiantes deberán acreditar su condición de tal (carnet escolar) y ser menores de 25 años.

INFORMACIONES Y VENTAS

- **Teatro Municipal** (Departamento de Ventas):
  San Antonio 191 esquina de Agustinas
  Lunes a viernes de 10:00 a 18:00 horas
  Fonos: 330752-332804-381722-381515-398200
- **Parque Arauco Shopping Center** (local 235):
  Lunes a sábado de 10:00 a 21:00 horas. Domingo de 11:00 a 21:00 horas.
  Fono: 2420930

Realia 5-1: Weather map

1. **Listening/Speaking:** Give students a place name and have them describe the weather there based on the information from the map.

2. **Listening:** Have students read over the weather map. Ask them to identify a place where the weather is warm, rainy, etc.

3. **Writing:** Have students write a description of the weather for their home city on a typical day.

4. **Pair work/Speaking:** Ask students to interview each other about which places on the map they would like to visit and why. The interview should include questions about why they would or would not like to visit based on the kinds of things they like to do.

Realia 5-2: Theater ad

1. **Listening:** Call out a date and ask students what programs they would be able to see on that date.

2. **Reading:** Ask students if they recognize the titles of the performances. Then ask them to read through each performance description and decide which program they would like to see.

3. **Reading:** After students have decided which programs they would like to see, ask them to decide where they would rather be seated.

4. **Listening/Speaking:** Give students various limitations. For example, tell them they are only able to go out on Saturday nights, or give them a specific amount of money to spend. Have them decide which performance and seating arrangement they would be able to choose.

5. **Pair work/Speaking:** Have pairs of students discuss the theatre ad and decide on a performance they would like to attend together. They should mention dates, times, prices, and where they want to sit.

6. **Group work:** Have small groups of students imagine that they are in charge of creating a similar ad for a theatre group. Have them decide together on a program, and then create an ad for that program.

Situation Cards 5-1, 5-2, 5-3: Interview

Situation 5-1: Interview

I am conducting a survey in order to know more about you and your classmates. I would like to know what things you do and how frequently you do them. Help me by answering the following questions.

¿Quiénes en la clase tocan la guitarra?
¿Quién cuida a su hermano/a durante la semana?
¿Ayudas en casa todos los días?
¿Con qué frecuencia hablas por teléfono?

Situation 5-2: Interview

I am a foreign visitor and I am curious about what you and your friends like to do together. How would you answer these questions?

¿Qué les gusta hacer durante el fin de semana?
¿Les gusta hacer ejercicio juntos?
¿Escriben cartas o miran la televisión los sábados por la noche?
¿Siempre leen las tiras cómicas los domingos?

Situation 5-3: Interview

My family is thinking about moving to your city. Can you give me some information about the weather?

¿Qué tiempo hace en la primavera?
¿Nieva mucho en el invierno?
¿Hace buen tiempo en el verano?
¿En qué meses hace calor?

Situation Cards 5-1, 5-2, 5-3: Role-playing

Situation 5-1 : Role-playing

Student A You and **Student B** want to compare how often you do certain activities. Choose three of the following activities and ask **Student B** how often he or she does them: ride a bike, study in the library, organize your room, spend time with friends, take the bus to school.

Student B You and **Student A** want to compare how often you do certain activities. Answer **Student A**'s questions and then find out how often he or she does three of the activities.

¿Con qué frecuencia? nunca siempre a veces

Situation 5-2: Role-playing

Student A Interview **Student B** and find out which of the following he or she likes to do: to read newspapers or magazines, to exercise or to scuba dive, to read the comics or to write postcards. Then answer **Student B**'s questions.

Student B Answer **Student A**'s questions, telling which you prefer. Then ask which of the following **Student B** likes: to fish or to ski, to run along the beach or to run in the park, to study or to do aerobic exercises.

¿Te gusta más...? pescar bucear leer revistas leer las tiras cómicas

Situation 5-3: Role-playing

Student A Pretend you are traveling to the United States for the very first time. You want to know what the weather is like in several cities during the spring and summer so you can decide which ones to visit. Ask **Student B** about the weather in the following places: Miami, Alaska, Chicago, San Antonio.

Student B **Student A** is traveling to the United States for the first time. Answer his or her questions about the weather in the spring and summer. Then switch roles.

¿Qué tiempo hace...? Llueve. Nieva.
Hace fresco. Hace mucho viento. Hace calor.

Student Response Forms

6 Escuchemos: Viejos amigos p. 129

Listen as Teresa tells Carlos what some of his old friends are doing. Match the name of each friend with when he or she works with Teresa.

_____ 1. Juan Luis	a. todos los días
_____ 2. Maite	b. los fines de semana
_____ 3. Alejandro	c. sólo cuando tiene tiempo los jueves
_____ 4. Flora	d. nunca
_____ 5. Ramón	e. siempre los lunes, a veces los jueves

9 Escuchemos: Mejores amigos p. 132

Gloria is writing an article about her best friends for the school newspaper. Listen as she interviews Carlos and Eddie. Then, for each activity shown on page 132 of your textbook, choose the best answer.

1. Les gusta _____.
2. No les gusta _____.
3. Sólo le gusta a Carlos _____.
4. Sólo le gusta a Eddie _____.

18 Escuchemos: Un día típico en la vida de... p. 136

Listen as Miguel's mother describes a typical day in his life, and decide which of these illustrations shows the real Miguel. Explain what is wrong with the incorrect illustrations.

a.

b.

c.

The real Miguel is pictured in ______.

______ is incorrect because ____.

______ is incorrect because ____.

23 Escuchemos: Meses y estaciones p. 139

Listen and match the date you hear with the correct picture.

a.

b.

c.

d.

e.

f.

1. ______
2. ______
3. ______
4. ______
5. ______
6. ______

Student Response Forms

Repaso Activity 1: p. 144

For each weather report you hear, determine which of the photos on page 144 of your textbook is being described.

1. ______
2. ______
3. ______
4. ______

Nombre ______________________ Clase ____________ Fecha ____________

CAPÍTULO 5 El ritmo de la vida

Quiz 5-1

Maximum Score: 30

PRIMER PASO

I. Listening

A. Listen as Ramón asks his friends questions. As they answer, write each friend's activity in Spanish. Use the infinitive form. Or check the appropriate column for how often he or she does it. (10 points)

	ACTIVITY	siempre	nunca	a veces	fines de semana
1. Luisa	desayunar				
2. Teresa					
3. Alejandro	lavar al perro				
4. Juan Luis	escuchar música				
5. Enrique					✓

SCORE

II. Reading

B. Clara and Diego are at a dance party, and Diego doesn't know much about some of the people. Read their conversation and respond with **sí** or **no** to the statements on p. 24. (10 points)

CLARA Hola, Diego. ¿Qué tal?

DIEGO Fantástico. Me gustan mucho los bailes. Pero no conozco (*I don't know*) a nadie. ¿Quién es la chica rubia?

CLARA Es Emilia. Es muy simpática y le gusta bailar también. Ella canta muy bien también. Le gusta mucho nadar y practicar deportes. Los fines de semana va a la piscina en el parque.

DIEGO Y los chicos morenos y altos, ¿quiénes son?

CLARA Son Miguel y Gustavo. Gustavo trabaja durante la semana, pero le gusta bailar los sábados. Miguel, en cambio (*on the other hand*), no trabaja. Ayuda en casa muchas veces y siempre prepara la cena durante la semana. Y tú, Diego, ¿qué haces?

DIEGO Nunca trabajo porque no tengo tiempo. Siempre estudio durante la semana, pero los sábados lavo el carro y cuido a mi hermana antes de pasar un rato con mis amigos. También monto en bicicleta los domingos. Y tú, Clara, ¿lavas el carro o cuidas a los hermanos?

CLARA Yo cuido a mi hermana a veces, pero nunca lavo el carro. Es muy aburrido lavar el carro. Pues, tengo que irme, Diego. Adiós.

DIEGO Adiós, Clara. ¡Que te diviertas mucho! (*Have fun!*)

Quiz 5-1

_____ 6. Clara habla con Emilia.

_____ 7. Emilia canta muy bien.

_____ 8. Emilia va a la piscina los lunes.

_____ 9. Miguel es bajo.

_____ 10. Gustavo trabaja los fines de semana.

_____ 11. Miguel trabaja en una tienda.

_____ 12. Diego no trabaja.

_____ 13. Diego ayuda en casa los sábados.

_____ 14. Diego estudia mucho.

_____ 15. Clara lava el carro sólo cuando no tiene tarea.

SCORE ____

III. Writing

C. Answer each of the following questions with a sentence. Using the cues in parentheses, say how often you do each thing. (10 points)

16. ¿Qué haces los sábados? (always)

____

17. ¿Con qué frecuencia desayunas? (at times)

____

18. ¿Qué haces para ayudar en casa? (every day)

____

19. ¿Quién lava la ropa en tu casa? (no one ever)

____

20. ¿Quiénes miran la televisión en tu casa? (often)

____

SCORE ____

TOTAL SCORE ____ /30

Nombre ____________________ Clase __________ Fecha __________

El ritmo de la vida

Quiz 5-2

SEGUNDO PASO

Maximum Score: 35

I. Listening

A. Listen to Luz ask questions about what her friends do. Match the answers that you hear to the appropriate pictures below. (10 points)

a.

b.

c.

d.

e.

1. _____ 2. _____ 3. _____ 4. _____ 5. _____

SCORE [ ]

II. Reading

B. Complete Mario's description of a typical day by filling in the blanks with words from the box. Not all words will be used, and no word will be used more than once. Capitalize words when necessary. (10 points)

a. nos	c. bebo	d. por la noche	g. encima	i. asisto	k. recibir
b. por la tarde		e. les	f. típicamente	h. corremos	j. como	l. me

6. __________ desayuno a las seis y media. 7. __________ jugo y luego me preparo para la escuela. Por la mañana 8. __________ a clases de matemáticas y computación. Luego, para el almuerzo, 9. __________ papas fritas y una hamburguesa con mis amigos.
10. __________ tengo una clase de baile con Elena y después 11. __________ gusta leer el periódico juntos. Después de clases, Elena y yo 12. __________ en el parque.
13. __________ cuando estoy en casa escribo cartas a mis amigos Tomás y Lolita en Miami. A ellos 14. __________ gusta 15. __________ muchas cartas porque están lejos de los amigos.

SCORE [ ]

Nombre ______________________ Clase ____________ Fecha ____________

Quiz 5-2

III. Writing

C. Write five sentences to describe what the people in the illustration are doing. (10 points)

16. ______________________

17. ______________________

18. ______________________

19. ______________________

20. ______________________

SCORE

IV. Culture

D. Based on the information in your textbook, respond to the statements below with **a) cierto** or **b) falso**. (5 points)

______ 21. In Spain and Latin America, most students have their own cars.

______ 22. Students in Latin America enjoy getting together with friends in public places.

SCORE

TOTAL SCORE /35

Nombre ______________________ Clase __________ Fecha __________

CAPÍTULO 5

El ritmo de la vida

CAPÍTULO 5

Quiz 5-3

TERCER PASO

Maximum Score: 35

I. Listening

A. Listen to descriptions of the weather for various places. Match what you hear to the appropriate pictures below. You may use a picture more than once. (10 points)

1. ______
2. ______
3. ______
4. ______
5. ______

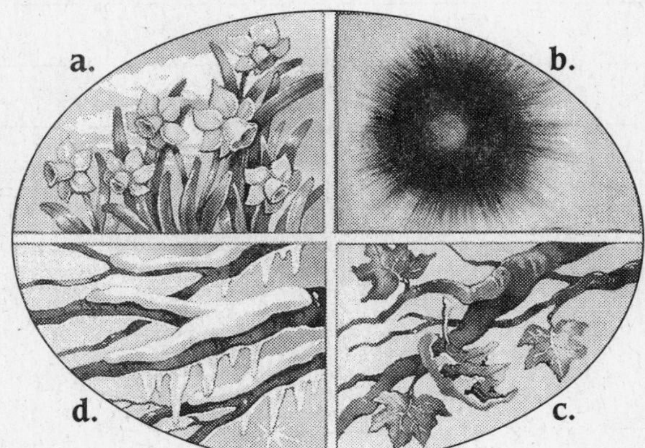

SCORE

II. Reading

B. Read the following statements about the weather, seasons, and months of the year in the Northern Hemisphere. If they are logical, write **sí**. If not, write **no**. (10 points)

______ 6. Hace calor. Es un día maravilloso para nadar.

______ 7. Es invierno y hace frío y nieva. Es ideal para esquiar.

______ 8. Hoy es el primero de agosto. Nieva mucho en Miami.

______ 9. Los meses del verano son septiembre, octubre y noviembre.

______ 10. Hace sol y es un buen día para ir a la playa.

______ 11. Está lloviendo. Es un día estupendo para caminar con el perro en el parque.

______ 12. Hoy es el primer día de la primavera. Es el veintidós de diciembre.

______ 13. En Nueva York, muchas personas van a la playa en diciembre.

______ 14. Los meses del otoño son marzo, abril y mayo.

______ 15. Hace frío y está nublado. Es un buen día para nadar.

SCORE

Nombre ______________________ Clase ____________ Fecha ____________

Quiz 5-3

III. Writing

C. In a short paragraph, describe your favorite time of the year. Include your favorite season, what you do, and describe the weather. Begin with **Mi estación favorita es...** (11 points)

16. ____

____

____

____

____

____

____

SCORE ____

IV. Culture

D. Based on the information in your textbook, respond with **a) cierto** or **b) falso** to the statements below. (4 points)

_____ **17.** In South America, summer begins in December.

_____ **18.** At the equator there are only two seasons.

SCORE ____

TOTAL SCORE ____ /35

CUMULATIVE SCORE FOR QUIZZES 1–3 ____ /100

CAPÍTULO 5

Nombre ______________________ Clase __________ Fecha __________

El ritmo de la vida

Chapter 5 Test

I. Listening

Maximum Score: 30 points

A. Listen as Tomás tells you about the pictures below. Write the letter of the picture he describes. (15 points)

a.

b.

c.

d.

e.

1. _____
2. _____
3. _____
4. _____
5. _____

SCORE

B. Beatriz and Memo are talking about things they like to do and how often they do them. Listen to their comments and decide what they do and don't have in common. Then, complete these statements about the two of them. (15 points)

6. A Beatriz le gusta ir a los restaurantes con sus amigos ________ a la semana.
   a. una vez **b.** dos o tres veces
7. Memo necesita ir al parque ________.
   a. los sábados **b.** todos los días
8. La actividad favorita de Memo es ________.
   a. esquiar **b.** correr
9. Los amigos van a ir a Colorado para las vacaciones de ________.
   a. primavera **b.** verano
10. A Memo le gusta mucho la nieve especialmente cuando ________.
    a. no hace mucho frío **b.** hace sol y frío al mismo tiempo

SCORE

Chapter 5 Test

II. Reading

Maximum Score: 30 points

C. Read what Julia has to say about what she and her friends think of spring and summer. Then indicate if the statements that follow are correct with **a) sí** or **b) no**. (12 points)

¡Qué buen tiempo hace en la primavera! A mis amigas y a mí nos gusta esta estación mucho. No nieva ni *(nor)* hace frío. Llueve a veces pero no hace calor—siempre hace fresco. Corremos por la playa todos los días, acampamos los fines de semana y pescamos muchas veces también. ¿Quién quiere asistir a clases o ayudar en casa cuando hace tan *(such)* buen tiempo? ¡Nadie! A todos les gusta pasar el rato con sus amigos al aire libre *(outdoors)*. Cuando llega el verano nadie quiere hacer nada. Mis amigas y yo nos quedamos *(remain)* en casa. Miramos la televisión, les escribimos cartas a nuestros amigos y leemos tiras cómicas. Nos gusta el verano sólo cuando nadamos en la piscina en el parque. A nosotras nos gusta más la primavera, especialmente durante los días de vacaciones.

_____ **11.** Julia and her friends prefer outdoor activities to indoor activities.

_____ **12.** Julia likes going to school in the spring.

_____ **13.** Julia likes to swim but her friends don't.

_____ **14.** Julia and her friends like spring better than summer.

SCORE

Chapter 5 Test 

D. José is filling out a questionnaire to find out if he exercises the right way. Write the letter of the best answer for each question. (18 points)

_____ **15.** Es importante correr. ¿Con qué frecuencia corre?
- **a.** Corres todos los días.
- **b.** Corro tres veces a la semana.
- **c.** Corro tres millas.

_____ **16.** Típicamente, ¿cuándo corre?
- **a.** Por la mañana, después del almuerzo.
- **b.** Por la tarde, después de mis clases.
- **c.** Por la noche, cuando hace sol.

_____ **17.** Cuando bucea, necesita compañeros. ¿Quiénes bucean con Ud.?
- **a.** Dos compañeros.
- **b.** No bucea.
- **c.** Yo buceo.

_____ **18.** Acampar es muy divertido. ¿Les gusta a Ud. y a sus amigos acampar?
- a. No, no les gusta.
- b. Sí, les gusta.
- c. No, no nos gusta.

_____ **19.** Las clases son muy importantes. ¿Asiste a una clase de ejercicios aeróbicos?
- a. No, sólo asisto a una clase de educación física.
- b. Sí, asisten a una clase de ejercicios aeróbicos.
- c. No, asistimos al colegio.

_____ **20.** La comida es muy importante también. ¿Qué come después de hacer ejercicio?
- **a.** Comemos hamburguesas.
- **b.** No como nada pero bebo mucha agua.
- **c.** Comen papas fritas.

SCORE ☐

III. Culture

Maximum Score: 9 points

E. Based on the information in your textbook, decide whether the following statements are **a) cierto** or **b) falso**. (9 points)

_____ **21.** Spanish-speaking teenagers often have weekday routines similar to those of teenagers in the United States.

_____ **22.** Spending time with groups of friends is unimportant in the lives of Spanish-speaking teens.

_____ **23.** Even though it is near the equator, the Andes region is cold because of its altitude.

SCORE ☐

Nombre ______________________ Clase ____________ Fecha ____________

Chapter 5 Test

IV. Writing

Maximum Score: 31 points

F. Based on the following pictures, write a sentence in Spanish to describe the weather on a particular day. Include the season or time of year in each sentence. (8 points)

24. ______________________________

25. ______________________________

26. ______________________________

27. ______________________________

SCORE

Chapter 5 Test 

G. Answer the questions below in complete sentences in Spanish. (14 points)

28. ¿Cuál es la fecha?

____

____

29. ¿Qué tiempo hace hoy?

____

____

30. ¿Cuáles son los meses del verano en los Estados Unidos?

____

____

31. ¿Cuándo hace frío en Miami?

____

____

32. ¿Qué les gusta hacer a ti y a tus amigos cuando hace calor?

____

____

33. ¿Con qué frecuencia escribes cartas en el invierno?

____

____

34. ¿Típicamente, hace más fresco por la mañana, por la tarde o por la noche?

____

____

SCORE [ ]

Chapter 5 Test

H. Write three sentences in Spanish telling what you like to do in at least three different seasons or weather situations. Include where, how often, and who you do the activities with. (9 points)

35. ____

____

36. ____

____

37. ____

____

SCORE [ ]

TOTAL SCORE [ ] /100

CAPÍTULO 5 Chapter Test Score Sheet

Circle the letter that matches the most appropriate response.

I. Listening

Maximum Score: 30 points

A. (15 points)

1. a b c d e
2. a b c d e
3. a b c d e
4. a b c d e
5. a b c d e

SCORE 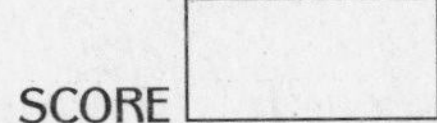

B. (15 points)

6. a b
7. a b
8. a b
9. a b
10. a b

SCORE

II. Reading

Maximum Score: 30 points

C. (12 points)

11. a b
12. a b
13. a b
14. a b

SCORE

D. (18 points)

15. a b c
16. a b c
17. a b c
18. a b c
19. a b c
20. a b c

SCORE

III. Culture

Maximum Score: 9 points

E. (9 points)

21. a b
22. a b
23. a b

SCORE

IV. Writing

Maximum Score: 31 points

F. (8 points)

24. ______

25. ______

26. ______

27. ______

SCORE

G. (14 points)

28. ______
29. ______
30. ______
31. ______
32. ______
33. ______
34. ______

SCORE

H. (9 points)

35. ______

36. ______

37. ______

SCORE

TOTAL SCORE /100

RESOURCES

Scripts and Answers

Additional Listening Activity 5-1, p. 11

ROQUE Hola, Ana María. Otra vez gracias por la entrevista.
ANA MARÍA De nada, hombre.
ROQUE Bueno, para comenzar... cuéntanos un poco de cómo es tu colegio en España. ¿Con qué frecuencia vas al colegio?
ANA MARÍA Voy al colegio de lunes a viernes, es decir, cinco días a la semana.
ROQUE ¿Y cuáles son algunas diferencias entre tu colegio en España y tu colegio aquí en los Estados Unidos?
ANA MARÍA Aquí los estudiantes siempre van a clases en autobús o en coche. En Santiago, nunca tomamos un bus para ir a clases. Vamos a pie.
ROQUE ¿Y qué otras diferencias hay?
ANA MARÍA Pues, en mi colegio siempre tenemos muchas clases... entre 8 y 9 materias típicamente. Aquí sólo tengo seis clases. Aquí en Estados Unidos, siempre hay muchísimos exámenes... prácticamente todas las semanas hay un examen en una de mis clases. ¡Es horrible! En mi colegio en España, siempre tenemos exámenes largos al fin del semestre, pero casi nunca tenemos exámenes así durante el semestre.
ROQUE ¿Y en España qué haces después de clases?
ANA MARÍA En España, después de clases, siempre voy con mis amigas a un café para tomar algo y comer algo. Casi nunca voy a casa directamente. Después, muchas veces paseamos en el parque o vamos todos a casa de un amigo.
ROQUE Bueno, Ana María, muchas gracias por la entrevista y que lo pases bien aquí en Miami.
ANA MARÍA Muchas gracias a ti. Me encanta todo, de verdad.

Additional Listening Activity 5-2, p. 11

LUIS Oye, Ana María, este viernes vamos al cine con Marta y Lola. ¿Quieres ir también?
ANA MARÍA ¿Marta y Lola? Mmmm... ¿quiénes son Marta y Lola?
LUIS Son compañeras de la clase de biología, ¿no te acuerdas? Muchas veces estudio con ellas en la biblioteca.
ANA MARÍA Ah, sí, claro.
LUIS Y el sábado hay una fiesta en casa de Héctor, a las ocho.
ANA MARÍA ¿Héctor juega al voleibol?
LUIS No, Héctor practica artes marciales. ¿Sabes? Es el presidente del Club de karate del colegio.
ANA MARÍA Claro, por supuesto. Pero si Héctor es el chico que practica karate, entonces... ¿quién juega al voleibol?
LUIS Creo que Miguel. Juega al voleibol en la playa todos los fines de semana. Es un jugador excelente.
ANA MARÍA Ah, sí... ahora recuerdo... sí. Se llama Miguel.
LUIS Y el domingo, si quieres, vamos a estudiar para el examen de literatura en casa de Sara.
ANA MARÍA ¿Quién es Sara?
LUIS Ay, Ana María... Sara es la presidenta del Club de drama. Es una actriz buenísima.
ANA MARÍA ¿Es una chica morena y delgada?
LUIS Sí, es Sara. Bueno, Ana María... ya conoces a todos los estudiantes. ¡Ahora necesitas memorizar y practicar todos los nombres!
ANA MARÍA Sí, necesito practicar mucho.

Additional Listening Activity 5-3, p. 12

RAMÓN ¿Qué hacemos mis amigos y yo en los ratos libres? Bueno, depende de la persona. A mis amigos Juan Carlos y Gabriela les gusta asistir a conciertos. Esta noche van a un concierto en el centro. A mí me gusta leer el periódico. Me gustan mucho las tiras cómicas y la sección de deportes. Mi amiga Sandra escribe artículos para el periódico del colegio. Ella quiere ser reportera en el futuro. A mis amigos Guillermo y Norma les gusta correr. Todos los días corren diez millas en la playa. ¡Diez millas! Increíble, ¿no? A mi amigo Pedro también le gustan los deportes, especialmente el basquetbol. Él asiste a todos los partidos de basquetbol de nuestro colegio. A mi amiga Cristina le gusta hacer ejercicio.

Additional Listening Activity 5-4, p. 12

TERESA Hola, a todos. Me llamo Teresa y les quiero explicar qué hago los sábados. ¿Cómo es un sábado normal para mí? Bueno... por la mañana, voy a la piscina con el resto del equipo de natación. Nadamos desde las ocho hasta las diez de la mañana. Regreso a casa y desayuno a las diez y media con mi familia. Siempre desayuno mucho: cereal, pan tostado, fruta, yogurt, jugo... ¡Qué rico! Por la tarde voy al trabajo. Todos los sábados trabajo en una clínica veterinaria. Siempre hay mucho que hacer en la clínica. Cuando regreso a casa, ayudo a preparar la cena. Después de cenar, a las ocho más o menos, mis amigos y yo vemos un video en casa, o vamos al cine.

Additional Listening Activity 5-5, p. 13

ELENA ¿Hola?
JAIME Hola, ¿eres tú, Elena? Habla Jaime.
ELENA Jaime, ¿qué tal?
JAIME Muy bien. ¿Y tú? ¿Cómo estás?
ELENA Bien, gracias. ¿Qué hay de nuevo?
JAIME Oye, ya sabes que hay muchas actividades esta semana y quiero saber si quieres ir a algunas conmigo. Por ejemplo, el lunes, el día once hay un concierto a las nueve. El miércoles, el día trece, hay una reunión del Club de español. Necesitas asistir a esa reunión porque vamos a tener elecciones para el presidente y el secretario.
ELENA De acuerdo. ¿A qué hora es la reunión?
JAIME A las cuatro de la tarde. Y el partido de basquetbol entre nuestro colegio y el Colegio Central es el domingo, el diecisiete. Ya sé que a ti te gustan los partidos de basquetbol.
ELENA ¿A qué hora es el partido? Generalmente visitamos a mis abuelos los domingos.
JAIME A las siete y media.
ELENA Ah, bueno, está bien. Sí, vamos juntos.
JAIME Y lo mejor de todo, el viernes, el quince, el mejor baile del año. ¡Va a ser increíble, con una banda musical y comida riquísima y todo! Es a las ocho y tienes que asistir.
ELENA Bueno, necesito hablar con mis padres. Quiero ir a todo.
JAIME Habla con tus padres, y después hablamos. Hasta luego.
ELENA Hasta luego, Jaime.

Additional Listening Activity 5-6, p. 13

LOCUTOR Muy buenas tardes, señoras y señores. Les habla Radio Onda Latina, la voz de la comunidad latina, desde el corazón de Miami. Hoy es viernes, el 9 de diciembre, y son las tres de la tarde. Les traigo el boletín meteorológico para hoy. Aquí en Miami hace mucho calor. Es un buen día para ir a la playa. En la ciudad de San Antonio, en el sur de Tejas, está lloviendo a cántaros. En Los Ángeles, hay un viento fuerte del Pacífico. En Denver, Colorado, está nevando—la tercera tormenta del año. En Boston hace sol. Y aquí termina el boletín meteorológico para las tres, señoras y señores. Que pasen Uds. buen fin de semana. Y ahora volvemos a nuestro programa musical para esta tarde.

Answers to Additional Listening Activities

Additional Listening Activity 5-1, p. 11

1. a
2. b
3. b
4. a
5. b

Additional Listening Activity 5-2, p. 11

1. c
2. d
3. e
4. a

Additional Listening Activity 5-3, p. 12

1. Juan Carlos y Gabriela: **asistir a conciertos**
2. Ramón: **leer el periódico**
3. Sandra: **escribir artículos**
4. Guillermo: y Norma **correr por la playa**
5. Pedro: **asistir a partidos de basquetbol del colegio**
6. Cristina: **hacer ejercicio**

Additional Listening Activity 5-4, p. 12

a. 4
b. 1
c. 3
d. 2

Additional Listening Activity 5-5, p. 13

lunes 11: concierto, 9:00 P.M.
miércoles 13: reunión del Club de español, 4:00 P.M.
viernes 15: baile, 8:00 P.M.
domingo 17: partido de basquetbol, 7:30 P.M.

Additional Listening Activity 5-6, p. 13

1. b
2. c
3. d
4. e
5. a

Quiz 5-1 Capítulo 5 Primer paso

I. Listening

A.
1. RAMÓN Oye, Luisa, ¿con qué frecuencia desayunas?
   LUISA ¿Yo? Siempre. Me gusta mucho la comida.
2. RAMÓN Y tú, Teresa, ¿siempre preparas la cena?
   TERESA No, pero los fines de semana preparo la cena en casa.
3. RAMÓN Alejandro, ¿te gusta lavar al perro a veces?
   ALEJANDRO Sí, a veces, pero no es divertido.
4. RAMÓN Y Juan Luis, ¿con qué frecuencia escuchas música?
   JUAN LUIS Pues, en realidad, no me gusta; nunca escucho música.
5. RAMÓN Enrique ¿todavía trabajas en la tienda los domingos?
   ENRIQUE Sí, y los sábados también.

Quiz 5-2 Capítulo 5 Segundo paso

I. Listening

A.
1. LUZ ¿Beben ustedes jugo de naranja, Mario y Alejandro?
   MARIO Sí, nos gusta mucho el jugo de naranja.
2. LUZ ¿Dónde les gusta hacer ejercicio a Mari y Chela?
   LUISA En el gimnasio.
3. LUZ ¿Qué hace Susana?
   ADRIANA Ella bucea en el lago.
4. LUZ ¿Qué hacen las chicas?
   MARCO Corren cinco millas por la playa.
5. LUZ ¿Les gusta a Uds. comer un sándwich o una ensalada para el almuerzo?
   JUAN Nos gusta comer un sándwich y beber leche.

Quiz 5-3 Capítulo 5 Tercer paso

I. Listening

A.
1. Hoy es el primero de enero en Nueva York. Hace mucho frío hoy.
2. Hace mucho sol en Miami porque estamos en pleno verano.
3. En Chicago es la primavera y hace mucho fresco.
4. Es un día perfecto para esquiar aquí en Colorado. Hace mucho frío y nieva.
5. Es otoño y hace fresco en Boston.

ANSWERS Quiz 5-1

I. Listening

A. (10 points: 2 points per item)
1. siempre
2. preparar la cena; fines de semana
3. a veces
4. nunca
5. trabajar en la tienda

II. Reading

B. (10 points: 1 point per item)
6. no
7. sí
8. no
9. no
10. no
11. no
12. sí
13. sí
14. sí
15. no

III. Writing

C. (10 points: 2 points per item)
Answers will vary. Possible answers:
16. Siempre ayudo a mi mamá. Lavo la ropa.
17. A veces desayuno durante la semana: los lunes, los miércoles y los viernes.
18. Todos los días preparo la cena, cuido a mi hermanito/a y saco la basura.
19. Nadie nunca lava la ropa en mi casa.
20. Mis hermanos miran la televisión muchas veces por la tarde.

ANSWERS Quiz 5-2

I. Listening

A. (10 points: 2 points per item)
1. e 2. c 3. d 4. a 5. b

II. Reading

B. (10 points: 1 point per item)
6. f
7. c
8. i
9. j
10. b
11. a
12. h
13. d
14. e
15. k

III. Writing

C. (10 points: 2 points per item)
Answers will vary. Possible answers:
16. Los Gómez caminan.
17. Ricardo y Julia corren.
18. Adriana come un sándwich.
19. Sandra come una hamburguesa.
20. María y Juan pescan.

IV. Culture

D. (5 points: 2 1/2 points per item)
21. b
22. a

ANSWERS Quiz 5-3

I. Listening

A. (10 points: 2 points per item)
1. d 2. b 3. a 4. d 5. c

II. Reading

B. (10 points: 1 point per item)
6. sí
7. sí
8. no
9. no
10. sí
11. no
12. no
13. no
14. no
15. no

III. Writing

C. (11 points)
Answers will vary. Possible answer:
16. Mi estación favorita es el otoño porque hace fresco y no hace mucho calor. No llueve ni nieva. Corro en el parque todos los días en el otoño.

IV. Culture

D. (5 points: 2 1/2 point per item)
17. a 18. a

Scripts for Chapter Test Capítulo 5

I. Listening

A.
1. En el invierno la chica esquía en Colorado.
2. Luis siempre nada cuando hace calor.
3. A veces Raquel y Armando almuerzan en la cafetería.
4. Los chicos corren en el parque en la primavera.
5. A Juanita le gusta escribir cartas en la biblioteca.

B.
BEATRIZ A mí me gusta mucho conocer gente nueva. Por eso me gusta ir a los restaurantes con mis amigos dos o tres veces a la semana.

MEMO ¡Sí, ya sé, Beatriz! Tú puedes pasar toda la semana en conversaciones con tus amigos. A mí eso no me gusta para nada. Necesito hacer muchas cosas. Yo necesito ir al parque a correr todos los días... ¡Pero esquiar es mi actividad favorita!

BEATRIZ Entonces, ¿por qué no vienes a Colorado con nosotros el cinco de marzo? Estamos planeando ir allá con Silvia y Fernando para las vacaciones de primavera.

MEMO ¡Perfecto! Me gusta mucho la nieve... especialmente cuando hace sol y frío al mismo tiempo.

Answers to Chapter Test

I. Listening Maximum Score: 30 points

A. (15 points: 3 points per item)
1. c
2. a
3. e
4. d
5. b

B. (15 points: 3 points per item)
6. b
7. b
8. a
9. a
10. b

II. Reading Maximum Score: 30 points

C. (12 points: 3 points per item)
11. a
12. b
13. b
14. a

D. (18 points: 3 points per item)
15. b
16. b
17. a
18. c
19. a
20. b

III. Culture Maximum Score: 9 points

E. (9 points: 3 points per item)
21. a
22. b
23. a

IV. Writing Maximum Score: 31 points

F. (8 points: 2 points per item)
Answers will vary. Possible answers:
24. Hoy es el primero de febrero y hace frío.
25. Hoy es el cuatro de julio. Hace calor y sol.
26. En invierno nieva mucho.
27. En la primavera hace mucho viento y llueve.

G. (14 points: 2 points per item)
Answers will vary. Possible answers:
28. Hoy es el (current date).
29. Hoy hace (calor, fresco...).
30. Los meses del verano son junio, julio y agosto.
31. Hace frío en Miami en enero.
32. Cuando hace calor, nos gusta (nadar, esquiar en el agua...).
33. Casi nunca escribo cartas en el invierno.
34. Hace más fresco por la noche.

H. (9 points: 3 points per item)
Answers will vary. Possible answers:
35. Durante la primavera me gusta correr en el parque con mi hermano.
36. Durante el invierno me gusta esquiar en las montañas con mis amigos.
37. Durante el otoño me gusta ir a fiestas con mis amigos.

El ritmo de la vida

DE ANTEMANO

1 Armando is a new student at Seminole High School in Miami. First read the letter he wrote to his cousin Yolanda in Panama about his new home and new routine, then answer the questions below.

Miami, 8 de noviembre

Querida Yolanda,

¿Cómo estás? Yo, muy bien. Aquí el ritmo de la vida es increíble. Hay muchísimas cosas que hacer en los ratos libres. Durante la semana, estoy muy ocupado. Los lunes y los jueves tengo la clase de artes marciales. Me gustan mucho el karate y el tae-kwon-do. Los martes tenemos la reunión del Club de arte de mi colegio. ¡Este año quiero ser presidente del club! Los miércoles y los viernes toco la batería en la banda del colegio. Tocamos en los partidos de fútbol todos los viernes por la noche. Los sábados por la noche, a veces vamos a una discoteca para bailar, o a una fiesta en casa de amigos. Los domingos, voy con mamá y papá a comer en un restaurante cubano. Pienso que la comida cubana es fantástica... a mis padres les gusta mucho también.

Bueno, escríbeme y cuéntame cómo están todos. Un fuerte abrazo para ti y para mis tíos.

Con cariño,
Armando

Look at Armando's schedule. Based on what he wrote in his letter, decide if all of the information is accurate. Check **sí** if it is correct. Check **no** if it is not. For the items that are not correct, fill in the calendar with the correct information.

		sí	no
lunes	*clase de artes marciales*	✓	
martes	*reunión del Club de español* **reunión del Club de arte**		✓
miércoles	*toca la batería con la orquesta* **toca la batería con la banda**		✓
jueves	*clase de arte* **clase de artes marciales**		✓
viernes	*toca la batería con la banda*	✓	
sábado	*va a la discoteca*	✓	
domingo	*va a un restaurante chino* **va a un restaurante cubano**		✓

Practice and Activity Book p. 49

PRIMER PASO

2 Xóchitl hasn't seen her grandmother for a while. Read the questions her **abuela** (*grandmother*) asks her, then write Xóchitl's responses, using the cues in parentheses. Follow the model.

MODELO Mi hija, ¡estás muy delgada! ¿No desayunas? (siempre)
Sí, abuela, siempre desayuno.

1. ¡Xóchitl! ¿Nunca organizas tu cuarto? ¡Es un desastre! (a veces)
   Sí, abuela. Organizo mi cuarto a veces.
2. Xóchitl, ¿todavía tocas el piano? Tócame (*Play me*) algo de Beethoven. (nunca)
   No, abuela, no toco el piano nunca./No, abuela, nunca toco el piano.
3. Xóchitl, ¿con qué frecuencia ayudas en casa? (todos los días)
   Ayudo en casa todos los días.
4. Xóchitl, ¿vas al cine con tus amigos durante la semana? (sólo cuando no tengo tarea)
   Sí, abuela, pero sólo cuando no tengo tarea.

3 Using the cues provided, write a true statement that each person might make using **siempre** or **no (nunca)**. Base your answers on what you know and on the cultural information you learned so far.

MODELO **Alma, Lawrence, Kansas:** tener nueve clases al día
Aquí nunca tenemos nueve clases al día.

1. **Juan, New York, New York:** regresar a casa a las doce del día para el almuerzo.
   Siempre regreso a casa a las doce para el almuerzo.
2. **Conchita, Oaxaca, México:** En el colegio, tener por lo menos (*at least*) ocho asignaturas.
   Nunca tengo ocho asignaturas en el colegio.
3. **Marcos, Valencia, España:** Para ir a la casa de un amigo, tomar el autobús.
   Para ir a la casa de un amigo, siempre vamos en coche. Nunca tomamos el autobús.
4. **Lourdes, San Ysidro, California:** En mi colegio, haber clases después de las tres y media de la tarde.
   En mi colegio, siempre hay clases hasta las cinco y media de la tarde.

Practice and Activity Book p. 50

4 What's it like to be a millionaire at sixteen? Read this interview between **Música y más** magazine and Adrián, a teenage star. Then respond to the statements that follow with **cierto** or **falso**. Correct the false statements.

Música y más entrevista a... *Adrián Sandoval*

M y m Seguro, Adrián, que no tienes tiempo para muchas cosas...

Adrián Bueno, ¡soy más normal de lo que piensas! (*I'm more normal than you think!*) Siempre tengo tiempo para mis amigos.

M y m Tienes una vida social muy ocupada (*a very busy social life*), ¿verdad?

Adrián A veces necesito cantar en conciertos o en programas de televisión. Pero, generalmente (*usually*), durante la semana estoy en casa.

M y m ¿Y cómo es un día típico?

Adrián Bueno, siempre desayuno. Después voy al colegio.

M y m ¡Qué bien! Y después del colegio, ¿qué haces?

Adrián A ver, a veces necesito trabajar en el estudio. Y necesito hacer la tarea todos los días.

M y m ¿Y los fines de semana?

Adrián Bueno, muchas veces no hago nada. Pero a veces me gusta ir con amigos a un restaurante o al cine, pero sólo cuando no tengo mucha tarea.

M y m Ya eres millonario, ¿no? ¿Y todavía ayudas en casa?

Adrián ¡Siempre! Muchas veces cuido a mis hermanos, y a veces aun (*even*) preparo la comida.

M y m ¿Y qué tal la comida que preparas?

Adrián ¡Horrible! ¡Guácala! (*Yuck!*)

1. Adrián no necesita cantar en conciertos todos los días.
   Cierto.
2. Muchas veces Adrián no desayuna porque está atrasado.
   Falso. Adrián desayuna todos los días.
3. Adrián siempre hace muchas cosas los fines de semana.
   Falso. A veces no hace nada.
4. Durante la semana va con amigos a un restaurante o al cine.
   Falso. Durante la semana está en casa.
5. Adrián siempre prepara la comida.
   Falso. A veces prepara la comida.

5 Make a list in Spanish of four things you never do, and explain why you never do them. Look at the vocabulary list for Chapter 5 if you need some ideas.

MODELO Nunca voy a los partidos de fútbol del colegio porque siempre trabajo los sábados por la mañana en el supermercado.

Answers will vary.

6 Who are your favorite people? Answer the questions below, explaining why each person or group of people is your favorite.

MODELO ¿Quién es tu persona favorita?
Mi "persona" favorita es mi perro Sam. No es una persona, pero es muy simpático y cómico.

1. ¿Quién es tu profesora favorita? **Answers will vary.** ____________
2. ¿Quién es tu cantante (*singer*) favorito? ____________
3. ¿Quién es tu mejor amigo o amiga? ____________
4. ¿Quiénes son tus atletas favoritos? ____________

7 What kind of life do you lead? Is it too busy, too disorganized, or just right? Take the following magazine poll to analyze your lifestyle. Answer each question based on what's true for you. Keep track of how many **a.**, **b.** and **c.** answers you've circled, and then read the article's description of your personality and lifestyle. Is it correct?

¿Te gusta el ritmo de tu vida?

1. ¿Con qué frecuencia haces la tarea?
a. siempre
b. a veces
c. nunca

2. ¿Con qué frecuencia descansas o duermes la siesta (*do you take a nap*)?
a. nunca o casi nunca
b. a veces
c. todos los días

3. ¿Con qué frecuencia organizas tu cuarto?
a. todos los días
b. sólo cuando sea (*it's*) necesario
c. nunca

4. ¿Con qué frecuencia vas al cine con tus amigos?
a. nunca
b. a veces
c. todos los días

5. ¿Con qué frecuencia lavas los platos?
a. todos los días
b. a veces
c. nunca

6. ¿Con qué frecuencia miras la televisión?
a. nunca
b. sólo a veces, para mirar mis programas favoritos
c. siempre

7. ¿Con qué frecuencia sacas la basura?
a. siempre
b. a veces
c. nunca

8. ¿Con qué frecuencia practicas un deporte?
a. nunca
b. a veces
c. todos los días

Análisis:

a.—Si la mayoría (*most*) de tus respuestas son **a.**, entonces trabajas mucho—¡y es un problema! Tienes un ritmo de vida muy acelerado y complicado. Necesitas tomar las cosas con más tranquilidad. Necesitas descansar más y hacer cosas divertidas en tus ratos libres.

b.—Si la mayoría de tus respuestas son **b.**, está bien. Eres una persona equilibrada. En tu vida hay un balance entre el trabajo, las responsabilidades y los ratos libres. Trabajas, pero también descansas.

c.—Si la mayoría de tus respuestas son **c.**, entonces descansas mucho—¡y es un problema! Tienes un ritmo de vida desorganizado. Necesitas ser más responsable y organizado en tu trabajo o en tus estudios. Recuerda que en la vida es importante tener un balance entre el descanso y el trabajo.

Practice and Activity Book p. 52

SEGUNDO PASO

8 Next year you will be an exchange student in Montevideo. Below is a letter from Clara, your host student, about what she and her friends like to do in their spare time. Read Clara's letter and complete it with the correct words or phrases from the box.

les	nos	te
a ellos		le
me		a ellos

Querido amigo,

¡Hola! Me llamo Clara Serrano, y soy de Montevideo, Uruguay. A mí 1. **me** *gustan muchas cosas: montar en bicicleta en el parque, comer pizza en el centro y pasar el rato con mis amigos. Después de clases, a nosotros* 2. **nos** *gusta ir al cine. A mi amigo Leonardo* 3. **le** *gustan las películas de aventuras. Mis amigas Carmen y Rebeca son simpáticas.* 4. **A ellas** *les gustan las películas de ciencia-ficción. Y qué curiosos son mis amigos Horacio y Abel.* 5. **A ellos** *les gustan mucho las películas de horror. Vamos al cine dos veces por semana. A mí* 6. **me** *gusta ir por la tarde, pero a mis amigos* 7. **les** *gusta ir por la noche. ¿A ti* 8. **te** *gusta ir al cine? ¿Qué películas* 9. **te** *gustan?*

9 For each of the drawings below, write a sentence explaining what the people pictured like, or don't like, to do. Then say how often they do the activities shown.

Marta y Susana

Isabel y Bingo

Joaquín y Laura

David y Micaela

1. **Answers will vary. Possible Answers: A Marta y a Susana no les gusta organizar su cuarto. No organizan su cuarto nunca.**
2. **A Isabel y a Bingo les gusta caminar en el parque. Isabel camina con Bingo todos los días.**
3. **A Joaquín y a Laura les gusta jugar al tenis. Juegan al tenis el martes y el sábado.**
4. **A David y a Micaela no les gusta jugar al voleibol en la clase de educación física. Tienen la clase los lunes y los miércoles.**

Practice and Activity Book p. 53

10 Imagine that you have a twin brother named Silvio. You both like to do many of the same things. Look at the lists of favorite activities for you and your twin. If only one of you likes an activity, write a sentence saying which one of you likes it. If you both like an activity, write a sentence saying that you like to do that activity together.

Yo	Silvio
esquiar	pescar
acampar	acampar
bucear	hacer ejercicio
correr por la playa	correr por la playa
hacer ejercicio	bucear

1. **A mí me gusta esquiar.**
2. **A Silvio le gusta pescar.**
3. **A nosotros nos gusta acampar juntos.**
4. **Nos gusta bucear juntos.**
5. **Nos gusta hacer ejercicio juntos.**
6. **Nos gusta correr por la playa juntos.**

11 The sentences below describe what some students and teachers at Seminole High School do in their free time. Complete the sentences with the correct forms of the verbs in parentheses, then check your answers by filling in the crossword puzzle with the missing words.

Horizontales

2. En la clase de literatura, nosotros ____ muchas novelas. (leer)
5. Todos los estudiantes ____ la reunión a las tres y media. (asistir a)
7. Martín y yo ____ un concierto este sábado. (asistir a)
9. Yo ____ una carta a mi amigo en La Habana todos los martes. (escribir)
10. Yo siempre ____ un sándwich en el almuerzo. (comer)
12. Santiago y Teresa ____ cartas cuando tienen tiempo. (escribir)
13. Nosotros ____ tacos en la cafetería del colegio los miércoles. (comer)

Verticales

1. Fátima y yo ____ una carta de España todos los sábados. (recibir)
2. Por la mañana, yo ____ el periódico en casa (leer).
3. Ricardo, ¿cuándo ____ la tarea, por la tarde o por la noche? (hacer)
4. ¿Qué ____ Elena después de clases? (hacer)
6. En la clase de historia, nosotros ____ composiciones. (escribir)
8. Nosotros siempre ____ agua después de correr. (beber)
10. El Sr. Guzmán y su perro Bobby ____ en el parque los fines de semana. (correr)
11. Germán y Lola ____ sus libros de texto en el autobús. (leer)

											[1]r					
									[2]l	e	e	m	o	s		
									e		c					
									o		i					
						[3]h					b					[4]h
						a			[5]a	s	i	s	t	e	n	a
						c					m					c
				[6]e		e					o					e
			[7]a	s	i	s	t	i	m	o	s	a				
				c												
				r				[8]b								
[9]e	s	c	r	i	b	o		e			[10]c	o	m	o		
				b				b			o					
				i		[11]l		[12]e	s	c	r	i	b	e	n	
				m		e		m			r					
			[13]c	o	m	e	m	o	s		e					
				s		n		s			n					

Practice and Activity Book p. 54

12 The planet Xargon has sent a team of investigators to find out about our planet and its inhabitants. You have been chosen to interpret the Xargonians' interviews for a Spanish-speaking audience. First write out the Xargonians' questions (items 1, 3, and 5). Then write what the earthlings answered, using expressions from the box below.

todos los días · sólo cuando... · muchas veces · durante... · a veces · por la mañana · siempre · por la noche · nunca · por la tarde

1. (The Xargonians want to know how often earthlings go to school.)
   Answers will vary. Some possible answers: ¿Con qué frecuencia van al colegio? ¿Van al colegio...?
2. **Voy al colegio todos los días, de lunes a viernes. Voy por la mañana y por la tarde.**
3. (The Xargonians want to know what students do after class.)
   ¿Qué hacen los estudiantes después de clase?
4. **Después de clase, muchas veces vamos al centro comercial o a la pizzería. A veces vamos al cine, o regresamos a casa.**
5. (The Xargonians want to know if students like to talk on the phone and how often.)
   ¿A tus amigos y a ti les gusta hablar por teléfono? ¿Con qué frecuencia?
6. **Sí, nos gusta hablar por teléfono. Hablamos sólo cuando no tenemos mucha tarea.**

TERCER PASO

13 By now you've learned how to talk about what day, month, and season it is in Spanish. Unscramble the words whose definitions appear below. If you unscramble each word correctly, you will find a message in the shaded vertical column.

MODELO **m a r z o** (El mes después de febrero)
r m a o z

1. **m i é r c o l e s** — e l m c é i o r s — El día entre (*between*) el martes y el jueves.
2. **o c t u b r e** — c r b e u o t — El mes antes de noviembre.
3. **s á b a d o** — b s d á a o — El día después del viernes.
4. **a b r i l** — i l b r a — El mes entre marzo y mayo.
5. **v e r a n o** — a v r o n a — La estación antes del otoño.
6. **m a r t e s** — s m e t r a — El día después del lunes.
7. **l u n e s** — e l n s u — El día después del domingo.
8. **p r i m a v e r a** — e r p a v i m a r — La estación antes del verano.
9. **f e c h a** — h a f c e — La palabra en español para *date*.
10. **i n v i e r n o** — v o n r i i e n — La estación antes de la primavera.
11. **d i c i e m b r e** — e r d m c b e i i — El mes después de noviembre.
12. **h o y** — y h o — El día antes de mañana.
13. **a g o s t o** — t a o g o s — El mes entre julio y septiembre.

14 Your pen pal Rosario from Perú wants to know about some U.S. holidays. Tell Rosario in what month the following special days fall this year.

1. El Día de la Independencia **El Día de la Independencia es el 4 de julio.**
2. El Día de Acción de Gracias (*Thanksgiving*) **El Día de Acción de Gracias es el ... de noviembre.**
3. El primer día del verano **El primer día del verano es 21 de junio.**
4. El Día de San Valentín **El Día de San Valentín es el 14 de febrero.**
5. El Año Nuevo **El Año Nuevo es el primero de enero.**
6. Tu cumpleaños (*birthday*) **Mi cumpleaños es el...**

Practice and Activity Book p. 56

15 It's easy to forget which season some months fall in! Read Javier's and Miguel's conversation, filling in the blanks with the correct seasons and months.

JAVIER Oye, Miguel, ¿cuál es tu estación favorita? La primavera, ¿verdad?

MIGUEL ¡Ya sabes que me gusta más el verano! Los meses de **junio**, **julio**, y **agosto**, cuando hace calor y voy a la piscina a nadar todos los días.

JAVIER Y el mes de septiembre, también, ¿no?

MIGUEL No, hombre. Septiembre es un mes de **otoño**.

JAVIER Ah, sí, tienes razón *(you're right)*. Con **octubre** y **noviembre**.

MIGUEL Y no te olvides de *(don't forget about)* diciembre.

JAVIER No, diciembre está en **el invierno**. También los meses de **enero** y **febrero**.

MIGUEL Y, por fin, **marzo**, **abril** y **mayo** son meses de **la primavera**.

16 For each of the illustrations below, write what season it is and what the weather is usually like where you live.

1. octubre — **Answers will vary. Possible answers: Es el otoño. Hace fresco.**
2. junio — **Es el verano. Hace sol.**
3. abril — **Es la primavera. Está lloviendo./Llueve./Está nublado.**
4. enero — **Es el invierno. Está nevando./Nieva./Está nublado.**
5. marzo — **Es la primavera. Hace mucho viento.**
6. julio — **Es el verano. Hace mucho calor.**

PRACTICE AND ACTIVITY BOOK CAPÍTULO 5 · ANSWERS

Practice and Activity Book p. 57

17 The weather can have a big effect on our daily activities. Look at the drawings of people below, and write one or two sentences describing what the people shown are doing or where they're going, and what the weather is like.

1. Elena y Sergio

2. El Sr. Jiménez

3. Susanita y Benjamín

4. Doña Blanca

1. **Elena y Sergio están en casa porque está lloviendo. Miran la televisión y comen sándwiches.**
2. **El Sr. Jiménez corre por la playa porque hace buen tiempo. No hace mucho viento.**
3. **Susanita y Benjamín van al parque para jugar porque hace viento.**
4. **Doña Blanca lee una novela y escucha música en casa porque está lloviendo y hace frío.**

18 What's your favorite time of year? Write a short paragraph of about eight lines in which you tell what season you like best and why. What's the weather like? What kinds of things do you and your friends like to do then?

Answers will vary.

Practice and Activity Book p. 58

VAMOS A LEER

19 Read the two comic strips, then answer the questions below.

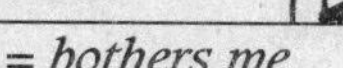

me molesta = *bothers me* **humedad** = *humidity* **salta** = *jump out*

tontas = *stupid* **asoleado** = *sunny* **regadera** = *watering can*
influir sobre sus mentes = *to play with their minds*

a. Check your comprehension by answering the following questions.

1. Why isn't Hobbes (the tiger) going to like the end of his wagon ride? ________________

   ____

2. How do you think Hobbes would describe Calvin in the last frame of the second strip? Write a caption in Spanish to express what he thinks of Calvin.

   ____

   ____

b. Read the following descriptions of Calvin and Hobbes and decide if they are accurate. If so, circle **sí**. If not, circle **no**. Then correct all of the information that is not accurate.

1. Calvin es alto, moreno y antipático. **sí** **(no)**
2. A Calvin no le gusta jugar. **sí** **(no)**
3. Hobbes es cómico, inteligente y simpático. **(sí)** **no**
4. A Calvin y Hobbes les gusta pasar el rato juntos. **(sí)** **no**

CULTURA

20 Based upon what you've learned about Spanish-speaking young people, correct the following statements if they are false.

1. It's fairly common for young people in Spain or Latin America to have their own cars.
   Falso. Young Spanish-speakers are more likely to take public transportation or walk.
2. Spanish-speaking young people often will make plans to meet friends in a park, a café or some other public place.
   Cierto
3. The streets of the average town or city in a Spanish-speaking country will most likely be deserted after sundown.
   Falso. People often go out at night and stay up rather late.
4. Young people in the Spanish-speaking world often tend to socialize in groups.
   Cierto

21 Imagine that you're a travel agent, specializing in trips to Latin America. What kind of clothing would you advise your customers to take with them if they're going to . . .? Explain briefly what the weather is like in each case.

1. make a trip to Argentina in December and January
   Answers will vary. Possible answers: summer clothes/ warm → hot weather
2. travel to southern Chile in mid-July
   winter clothes
3. take a tour of the Andean region of Ecuador in May
   warm clothes

22 Imagine that you're going to spend the month of January in Buenos Aires, Argentina. Through an exchange program, you'll be living with an Argentine family with two kids your age. In this chapter you've read about Spanish-speaking young people and about the climate in southern South America. Based on what you've learned in this chapter, what might you expect to see and experience with your host family in Buenos Aires?

Answers will vary.

Practice and Activity Book p. 60

VAMOS A LEER

3 A los detalles

1. Es una combinación de valores hispanos y del modo de vida americano.
2. Los padres de Sony llegaron a los Estados Unidos sin hablar el inglés.
3. Nunca han estado en un medio donde el dominio del inglés haya sido una exigencia.
4. A veces se siente abrumado.
5. Quiere asistir a la universidad y obtener su título. Después quiere encontrar un buen empleo.

4 Vamos a comprenderlo bien

1. La familia depende del hijo bilingüe para cumplir sus necesidades cotidianas.
2. *Answers will vary.*
3. *Answers will vary.*
4. *Answers will vary.*
5. *Answers will vary.*

5 Reglas de acentuación: las palabras agudas

1. n
2. n, s
3. a.
4.

cartón	amistad	cartel	dormir
cortés	**atrás**	pared	**sillón**
José	cultural	tomar	**pronunciación**
papel	**canción**	**francés**	juventud

6 Ortografía: las letras c, s y z

1.

z	s	c
razón	dieciséis	oficial
aprendizaje	sus	cubanoamericano
fuerza	hispanos	formación
	social	cuentan
	sido	compras
	estado	nunca
	casa	encendido
	presentan	autosuficiente
	asistir	cajero

2. La c y la z se pronuncian a veces en forma paedica, por ejemplo: ra*zón* y so*cial*. Pero a veces la c se pronuncia como una k, por ejemplo: casa.
3. Cuando la letra c es seguida por las letras e o i en una palabra, se pronuncia como la s. Por ejemplo: die*ci*séis y en*cen*dido.
4. Hay que tomar en cuenta los sonidos de las vocales que siguen a la consonante para observar su pronunciación. Por ejemplo, cuando a la c le siguen los sonidos a, o u u, se pronuncia fuerte, como si fuera una k.

5. hizo
hazme
empecé
empezó

VAMOS A ESCRIBIR

7 *Answers will vary.*

VAMOS A CONOCERNOS

8 A escuchar

Answers will vary.

9 A pensar

Answers will vary.

10 Así lo decimos nosotros

Palabra inglesa	Variante local	Español internacional
house	cantón	**casa**
friend	**cuate**	amigo
to quit	cuitear	renunciar
competition	competición	**competencia**
shoes	zapos	zapatos
classroom	clecha	**salón de clase**
yes	**simón**	sí
truck	troca	**camión**

VAMOS A CONVERSAR

11 *Answers will vary.*

Entre familia

RESOURCES

CAPÍTULO 6

Entre familia

Chapter Teaching Resources Correlation Chart

RESOURCES	Print	Audiovisual
De antemano	*Practice and Activity Book*, p. 61	
	Video Guide OR *Videodisc Guide*	*Textbook Audiocassette 3B/Audio CD 6* *Video Program* OR *Expanded Video Program, Videocassette 2* OR *Videodisc Program, Videodisc 3B*
Primer paso	*Chapter Teaching Resources, Book 2*	
	• Teaching Transparency Master 6-1, p. 65	*Teaching Transparency 6-1*
	• Additional Listening Activities 6-1, 6-2, p. 69 —Scripts, p. 96; Answers, p. 98	*Additional Listening Activities, Audiocassette 9B/Audio CD 6*
	• Realia 6-1, pp. 73, 75	
	• Situation Cards 6-1, pp. 76–77	
	• Student Response Forms, p. 78	
	• Quiz 6-1, pp. 81–82 —Scripts, p. 99; Answers, p. 100	*Assessment Items, Audiocassette 7B/Audio CD 6*
	Practice and Activity Book, pp. 62–64 —Answers: *Chapter Teaching Resources, Book 2*, pp. 104–106	
	Native Speaker Activity Book, pp. 26–30 —Answers: *Chapter Teaching Resources, Book 2*, pp. 115–116	
	Videodisc Guide	*Videodisc Program, Videodisc 3B*
	Video Guide	*Video Program* OR *Expanded Video Program, Videocassette 2*
Segundo paso	*Chapter Teaching Resources, Book 2*	
	• Communicative Activity 6-1, pp. 61–62	
	• Teaching Transparency Master 6-2, p. 66	*Teaching Transparency 6-2*
	• Additional Listening Activities 6-3, 6-4, p. 70 —Scripts, p. 96; Answers, p. 98	*Additional Listening Activities, Audiocassette 9B/Audio CD 6*
	• Realia 6-2, pp. 74, 75	
	• Situation Cards 6-2, pp. 76–77	
	• Student Response Forms, p. 79	
	• Quiz 6-2, pp. 83–84 —Scripts, p. 99; Answers, p. 100	*Assessment Items, Audiocassette 7B/Audio CD 6*
	Practice and Activity Book, pp. 65–67 —Answers: *Chapter Teaching Resources, Book 2*, pp. 107–109	
	Native Speaker Activity Book, pp. 26–30 —Answers: *Chapter Teaching Resources, Book 2*, pp. 115–116	
	Videodisc Guide	*Videodisc Program, Videodisc 3B*
Tercer paso	*Chapter Teaching Resources, Book 2*	
	• Communicative Activity 6-2, pp. 63–64	
	• Teaching Transparency Master 6-3, p. 67	*Teaching Transparency 6-3*
	• Additional Listening Activities 6-5, 6-6, p. 71 —Scripts, p. 97; Answers, p. 98	*Additional Listening Activities, Audiocassette 9B/Audio CD 6*
	• Realia 6-2, pp. 74, 75	
	• Situation Cards 6-3, pp. 76–77	
	• Student Response Forms, p. 80	
	• Quiz 6-3, pp. 85–86 —Scripts, p. 99; Answers, p. 100	*Assessment Items, Audiocassette 7B/Audio CD 6*
	Practice and Activity Book, pp. 68–70 —Answers: *Chapter Teaching Resources, Book 2*, pp. 110–112	
	Native Speaker Activity Book, pp. 26–30 —Answers: *Chapter Teaching Resources, Book 2*, pp. 115–116	
	Videodisc Guide	*Videodisc Program, Videodisc 3B*

ASSESSMENT

Paso Quizzes
- *Chapter Teaching Resources, Book 2*
  Quizzes pp. 81–86
  Scripts and answers pp. 99–100
- Assessment Items, *Audiocassette 7B/Audio CD 6*

Portfolio Assessment
- *Assessment Guide*, pp. 2–13. 19

Chapter Test
- *Chapter Teaching Resources, Book 2*, pp. 87–92
  Test score sheets, pp. 93–94
  Test scripts and answers, pp. 101–102
- *Assessment Guide*, Speaking Test, p. 30
- Assessment Items, *Audiocassette 7B/Audio CD 6*

Test Generator, Chapter 6

Communicative Activity 6-1 A

1. You and your partner are cousins trying to complete this family tree. Using the family tree below, ask your partner questions to fill in any missing information and answer your partner's questions with the information provided. When you have both finished, compare your family trees to see if they are the same.

MODELO — **¿Cómo se llama la madre de Catalina?**
— **¿Cómo se llama el hermano de Tomás?**

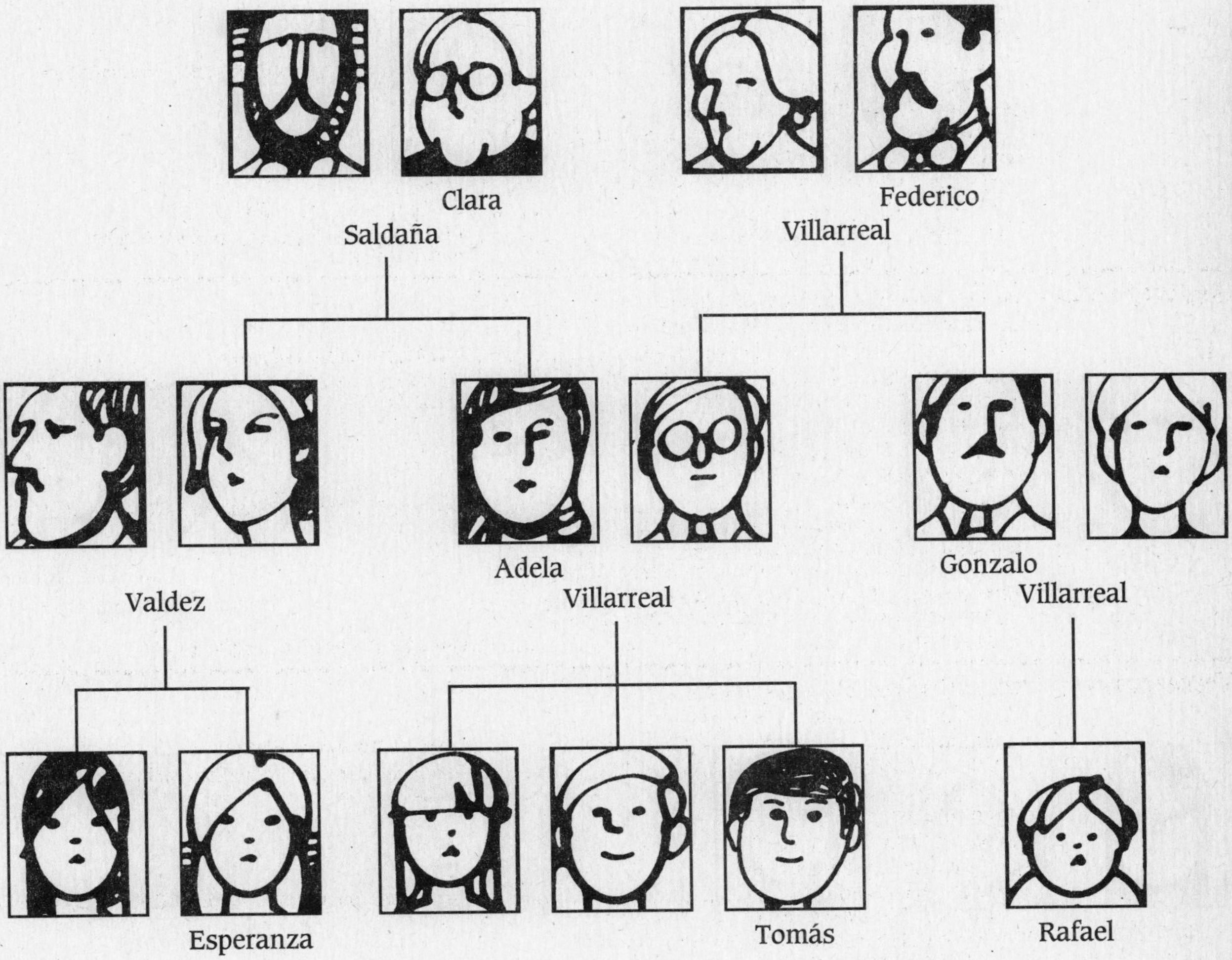

Clara
Saldaña

Federico
Villarreal

Adela
Valdez

Villarreal

Gonzalo
Villarreal

Esperanza

Tomás

Rafael

Nombre ______________________ Clase __________ Fecha __________

Communicative Activity 6-1 B

1. You and your partner are cousins trying to complete this family tree. Using the family tree below, ask your partner questions to fill in any missing information and answer your partner's questions with the information provided. When you have both finished, compare your family trees to see if they are the same.

MODELO — **¿Cómo se llama la madre de Catalina?**
— **¿Cómo se llama el hermano de Tomás?**

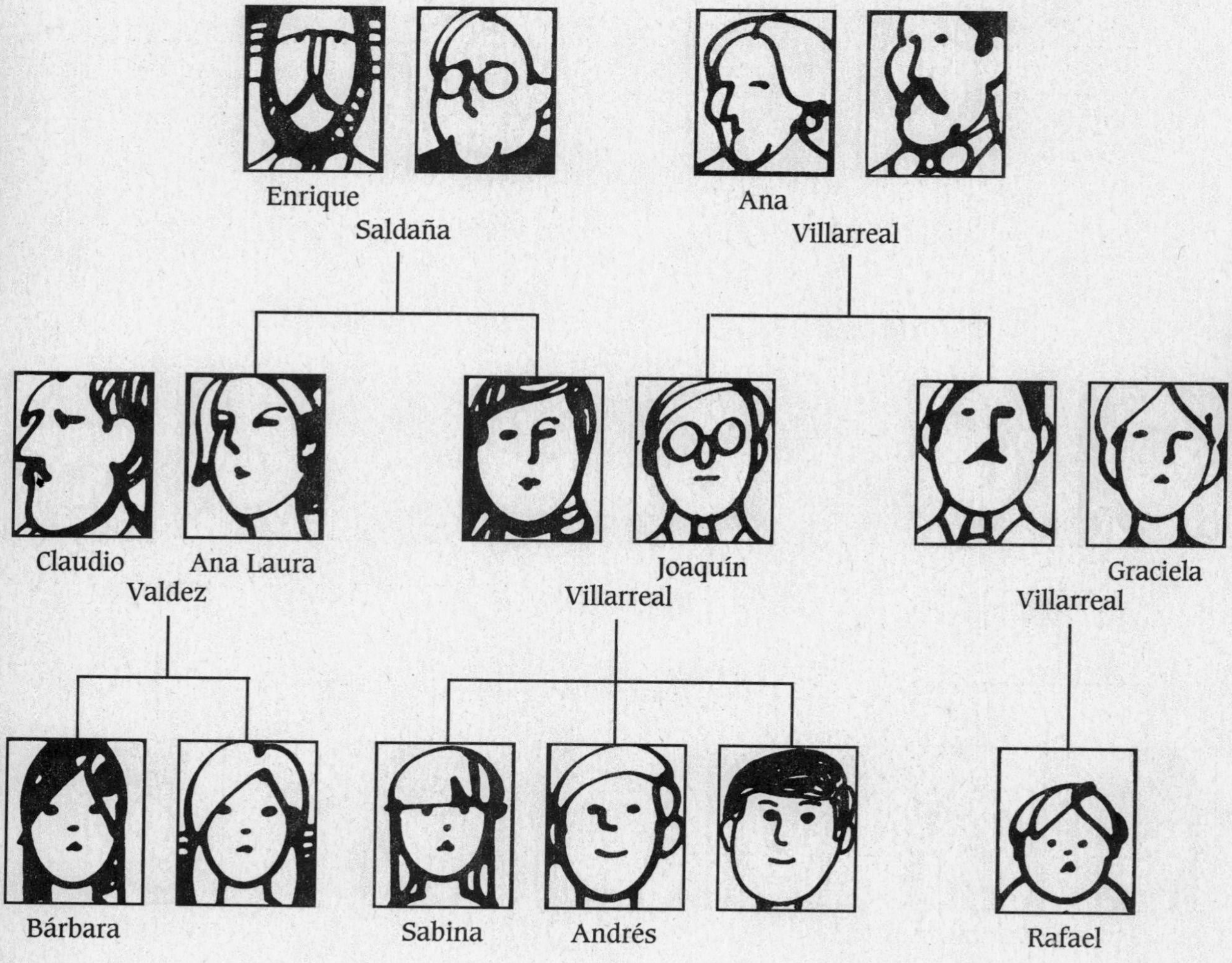

Enrique
Saldaña

Ana
Villarreal

Claudio
Valdez
Ana Laura

Joaquín
Villarreal

Graciela
Villarreal

Bárbara

Sabina

Andrés

Rafael

CAPÍTULO 6

Nombre ______________________ Clase ____________ Fecha ____________

Communicative Activity 6-2A

1. You and a group of friends have been hired to clean the house belonging to Madame Anastasia, the mysterious elderly Russian lady living down the street. You're in charge of the upstairs (**arriba**) and your partner is in charge of the downstairs (**abajo**) and outside of the house (**afuera**). Madame Anastasia has already decided which of you and your friends will do the various tasks. You have the downstairs list and your partner has the upstairs list. Fill in the chart below by asking your partner what each of your friends should do.

MODELO — **¿Qué debe hacer María?**
— **María debe poner la mesa.**

Arriba...

NOMBRE	**Santiago**	**Alicia**	**Oralia**	**Jaime**	**Eduardo**
QUEHACER					

CAPÍTULO 6

2. Now answer your partner's questions about which downstairs and outside task each of your friends should do.

Abajo y afuera...

NOMBRE	**Orieta**	**Beatriz**	**Roberto**	**Rosana**	**Enrique**
QUEHACER				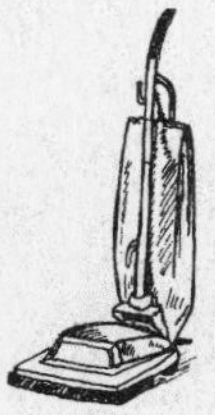	

Communicative Activity 6-2B

1. You and a group of friends have been hired to clean the house belonging to Madame Anastasia, the mysterious elderly Russian lady living down the street. You're in charge of the downstairs (**abajo**) and outside of the house (**afuera**), and your partner is in charge of the upstairs (**arriba**). Madame Anastasia has already decided which of you and your friends will do the various tasks. You have the downstairs list and your partner has the upstairs list. Answer your partner's questions about what each of your friends should do.

MODELO — **¿Qué debe hacer María?**
— **María debe poner la mesa.**

Arriba...

NOMBRE	Santiago	Alicia	Oralia	Jaime	Eduardo
QUEHACER					

2. Now, to fill in the chart below, ask your partner which downstairs and outside task each of your friends should do.

Abajo y afuera...

NOMBRE	Orieta	Beatriz	Roberto	Rosana	Enrique
QUEHACER					

Nombre ______________________ Clase ____________ Fecha ____________

Teaching Transparency Master 6-1

Rolando
- 70 -

Cecilia
- 69 -

Elena
- 42 -

Mario
- 41 -

Rosa
- 36 -

Miguel
- 38 -

Mónica
- 18 -

Édgar
- 15 -

Eric
- 10 -

Valeria
- 16 -

Víctor
- 8 -

Nombre ______________________ Clase ______________ Fecha ______________

Teaching Transparency Master 6-2

Nombre ______________________ Clase ______________ Fecha ______________

Teaching Transparency Master 6-3

Using Teaching Transparencies 6-1, 6-2, 6-3

Teaching Transparency 6-1

1. **Speaking:** Ask students to identify the relationship between various people in the tree. For example. **¿Quién es el abuelo de Eric?**
2. **Speaking:** Have students describe various people in the family. Have them give a physical description as well as what they like and don't like.
3. **Listening:** Give a description of a particular family member and have students identify the person you're describing. Include age, likes, and dislikes.
4. **Pair work/Writing:** Have pairs of students draw a family tree based on an imaginary family. For each member they should include age and some likes and dislikes.
5. **Listening/Speaking:** Offer students (especially native speakers) an opportunity to talk about even more extended family relationships. Teach the words **nuera, yerno, cuñados, nietos, sobrinos,** and **suegros.** Explain the importance of these relationships in Spanish-speaking cultures.

Teaching Transparency 6-2

1. **Speaking:** Have students assign a name to the various family members in the transparency. Have them describe the person and have students guess who is being described.
2. **Listening/Speaking:** Have students tell what each family is doing together.
3. **Writing:** Have students write about what they and their families do together. They may use their own families or an imaginary one.
4. **Pair or Group work:** Have pairs or small groups of students think of a problem (for example, someone forgot to bring some important object, or someone forgot to make reservations). Students should create a conversation in which the people illustrated attempt to deal with the problem.

Teaching Transparency 6-3

1. **Listening:** Describe a particular room and have students tell you which room you're describing. Give them the impersonal **se** and use phrases such as **aquí se necesita pasar la aspiradora**.
2. **Speaking:** Have students make a list for a professional cleaning company of chores that need to be done in the house.
3. **Pair work/Speaking:** Have students discuss in pairs the chores they like and don't like to do. Have them also talk about what chores other members of their families like and don't like to do.
4. **Writing:** Have students write a list of the things that they are supposed to do around the house using the verb **deber**. They may base their list on their own home or an imaginary one.

Nombre ______________________ Clase ____________ Fecha ____________

Additional Listening Activities

PRIMER PASO

6-1 You will hear a description of Susana's family. As you listen, write the names and ages of her relatives in the spaces below their pictures.

CAPÍTULO 6

6-2 Listen as your friend Luisa talks about her family. Then choose the answer that best completes each statement according to her description.

1. Luisa tiene una familia ____.
   a. grande
   b. pequeña

2. Sus abuelos tienen ____.
   a. un gato y un perro
   b. dos gatos

3. Luisa tiene tres ____.
   a. hermanos mayores
   b. primos

4. Cada domingo su familia ____.
   a. visita a sus abuelos
   b. va al parque

Additional Listening Activities

SEGUNDO PASO

6-3 Listen as these teenagers talk about what they do on the weekends with their families. Listen to their descriptions and match each one with the correct picture. One description will not have a matching picture.

_____ **1.** Pedro

_____ **2.** Alicia

_____ **3.** Esteban

_____ **4.** Paula

a.

b.

c.

6-4 Patricia and Tomás Acosta are trying to figure out when they can go shopping for a present for their mom's birthday on Saturday. Listen to their conversation and decide when they can go together.

____

Nombre ______________________ Clase ____________ Fecha ____________

TERCER PASO

6-5 While Sra. Acosta is out running errands, everyone else in the Acosta house is getting ready for the big surprise birthday party for her this evening. Listen to the description of who is doing what and write what each person is doing next to his or her name.

1. Doña Rebeca ______________________
2. Sr. Acosta ______________________
3. Anita ______________________
4. Tomás ______________________

6-6 The Ramos children are staying with tío Ricardo while their parents look for a new place to live. Tío Ricardo works all day and is advising all his nephews and nieces what they will need to do to help out around the house.

____

____

____

____

____

____

____

____

Nombre ______________________ Clase ______________ Fecha ______________

Additional Listening Activities

SONG

This lovely song was written by the Cuban poet, essayist, and patriot José Martí (1853-1895). In this song about a peasant girl from the city of Guantánamo, one can sense Martí's pride in and love for the life of the common people.

***Guantanamera** (Cuba)*

Guantanamera, guajira guantanamera,
guantanamera, guajira guantanamera.

Yo soy un hombre sincero,
de donde crece la palma,
y antes de morirme quiero,
echar mis versos del alma.

Guantanamera, guajira guantanamera,
guantanamera, guajira guantanamera.

Mi verso es de un verde claro,
y de un carmín encendido;
mi verso es un ciervo herido,
que en el monte busca amparo.

Guantanamera, guajira guantanamera,
guantanamera, guajira guantanamera.

Con los pobres de la tierra,
quiero yo mi suerte echar;
el arroyo de la sierra,
me complace más que el mar.

Guantanamera, guajira guantanamera,
guantanamera, guajira guantanamera.
guarija guantanamera, etc...

This song is recorded on *Audio CD 6* and also on *Audiocassette 11: Songs*. Although it is presented in this chapter, it can be used at any time.

Recuerdo de Bautizo

Pablo Ricardo Pérez García
nació el 25 de junio de 1986

Los padres:
Marcos Santos Pérez
y
María García de Pérez

Los padrinos:
Francisco Delgado
y
Graciela García de Delgado

Fue bautizado
en la Santa Catedral de
nuestra Señora de la Luz
en Valparaíso, Chile
el día 29 de julio
de 1986

Te invito a celebrar mi

PRIMERA COMUNION

el día 5 de mayo de 1994
en
La Iglesia de Nuestro Salvador
a la 1 de la tarde
Espero verte sin falta
Pablo Ricardo Pérez García

Realia 6-2

Realia 6-1: Baptismal and Communion invitations

1. **Listening:** Before distributing copies to students, read each of the announcements aloud to see if they can guess what the topic is.

2. **Reading:** Ask students the meanings of several words such as **nació, recuerdo,** and **bautizado**. Ask them if they can guess the tense of **nació**.

3. **Writing:** Have students write an invitation to a ceremony or celebration of their own. It can be a religious ceremony, a birthday party, or a holiday celebration.

4. **Pair work/Speaking:** Ask pairs of students to pretend that it is their job to select godparents for a new baby in their (imaginary) family. Have them discuss the responsibilities involved and consider several people in the "family" who might do a good job. Have them present their final choices to the class and explain why they chose them.

Realia 6-2: Housecleaning service ad

1. **Listening:** Before distributing copies to students, read the ad aloud to see if they can guess the topic of the ad.

2. **Listening/Reading:** Call out a specific household chore and ask the students if this ad offers that service.

3. **Speaking:** Have students name all the household chores that this ad offers.

4. **Writing:** Have students write their own announcement advertising their own housecleaning service or some other service.

Situation Cards 6-1, 6-2, 6-3: Interview

Situation 6-1: Interview

Tell me about your family or an imaginary one.

¿Cuántas personas hay en tu familia?
¿Quiénes son?
¿Tienen Uds. un perro o un gato?
¿Quién en tu familia es cómico?

Situation 6-2: Interview

Think of a person you know well and really like and answer my questions about that person.

¿Cómo se llama tu amigo/a?
¿Cuántos años tiene?
¿De qué color son los ojos?
¿Cómo es? Por ejemplo, ¿es travieso o cómico?

Situation 6-3: Interview

I need your advice. Tell me what I should do in each situation.

Tengo un examen mañana en la clase de biología, pero quiero salir con mis amigos. ¿Qué debo hacer?
Mis abuelos van a visitar esta noche, pero la casa es un desastre. ¿Qué debemos hacer?
Quiero ir al centro comercial con mi amigo, pero tengo mucha tarea. ¿Qué debo hacer?

Nombre ______________________ Clase ____________ Fecha ____________

Situation Cards 6-1, 6-2, 6-3: Role-playing

Situation 6-1 : Role-playing

Student A You and **Student B** are talking about your families, real or imaginary. Ask **Student B** if he or she has a large or small family. Also find out how many brothers and/or sisters **Student B** has. Ask if he or she has a cat or dog. Then answer **Student B**'s questions.

Student B You and **Student A** are talking about your real or imaginary families. Answer **Student A**'s questions about your family and then ask him or her how many people are in his or her family. Also ask how old his or her brothers and/or sisters are.

¿Tienes...? **¿Cuántos/as?**

Situation 6-2: Role-playing

Student A Imagine you are talking long distance to **Student B** who is an exchange student coming to live with you soon. Introduce yourself and give **Student B** a detailed description of yourself and your personality. Then ask **Student B** what he or she is like.

Student B Imagine you are an exchange student talking long distance to **Student A** who soon will be your host in the U.S. Listen to his or her description and then answer **Student A**'s question.

Tengo... **los ojos** **travieso/a** **cariñoso/a**

Situation 6-3: Role-playing

Student A You and **Student B** are comparing the things you have to do around the house to help out. Tell **Student B** two chores that you do and then ask **Student B** what he or she does.

Student B You and **Student A** are comparing chores you do around the house. Listen to what **Student A** does and then answer his or her question, telling two or three things you do to help out.

lavar **limpiar** **pasar la aspiradora**

Nombre ______________________ Clase ____________ Fecha ____________

Student Response Forms

6 Escuchemos: ¿Quién es quién? p. 153

Imagine that you're on the phone with the photographer who took the family portraits above. As she describes members of each family, find the picture that matches. If no picture matches, answer **ninguna foto**.

1. ______
2. ______
3. ______
4. ______
5. ______

CAPÍTULO 6

15 Escuchemos: ¿Ciencia ficción? p. 158

Listen to the following descriptions of some fictional characters and use **probable** and **improbable** to tell what you think of their appearances.

1. ____________________
2. ____________________
3. ____________________
4. ____________________
5. ____________________
6. ____________________

16 Escuchemos: ¿Cómo son tus amigos? p. 159

Listen as Rogelio describes some people and his cat to his Aunt Maki. Using the illustrations on page 159 of your textbook, identify each character by name. Does Maki know one of them especially well?

1. ______________________
2. ______________________
3. ______________________
4. ______________________
5. ______________________

The person she knows especially well is ______________________.

21 Escuchemos: Con la familia p. 160

Listen as four friends discuss what they do with their families and friends. Match the description you hear with the correct photo on page 160 of your textbook.

1. ______
2. ______
3. ______
4. ______

Student Response Forms

28 Escuchemos: Los problemas de Mónica p. 164

Listen as Mónica describes her family. Then match the pictures on page 164 of your textbook to the correct description you hear. One of the people she describes isn't pictured. Who is it?

1. Mónica — a. ______
2. su mamá — b. ______
3. su hermana menor — c. ______
4. su tía — ______________ is not pictured.

Repaso Activity 1 p. 170

First read the statements below about Marcos and his family. Then listen as Marcos describes his family in detail. Decide which family member matches each numbered item below.

1. Debe comer menos. ______________________
2. Trabaja demasiado. ______________________
3. Lee muchas novelas. ______________________
4. Tiene un cuarto muy organizado. ______________________
5. Le gusta tocar la guitarra. ______________________
6. No estudia mucho. ______________________

Nombre ______________________ Clase ____________ Fecha ____________

Entre familia

Quiz 6-1

PRIMER PASO

Maximum Score: 35

I. Listening

A. Carlos is telling Margarita about his family relationships. Look at the family tree below and answer **sí** or **no** to indicate whether his statements are accurate or not. (10 points)

1. ______
2. ______
3. ______
4. ______
5. ______

Mario, Luisa, José, Pilar, Juana, Julio, Rosa, Pedro, Elena, Julia, Carlos (yo), Laura, Jaime

SCORE

II. Reading

B. Antonio is with María at a family party. He doesn't know many of her relatives. Read their conversation and then respond with **sí** or **no** to the statements that follow. (8 points)

ANTONIO ¿Cuántas personas hay en tu familia?
MARÍA Hay muchas. Nuestra familia es grande.
ANTONIO ¿Quién es el chico alto?
MARÍA Es mi hermano José.
ANTONIO ¿Y la chica rubia y bonita que está a su lado?
MARÍA Es mi prima Inés. Es muy simpática. Ella tiene tres hermanos: Juan, Isabel y Bárbara. Isabel y Bárbara son muy cómicas e inteligentes también.
ANTONIO ¿Y el señor moreno y alto? ¿Es tu padre?
MARÍA No, es Gregorio, mi padrastro. Es muy simpático.
ANTONIO ¿Y la chica baja y rubia?
MARÍA Es Clara, la hija de Gregorio. Es mi hermanastra.

______ 6. El hermano de María es alto.

______ 7. María y Antonio son hermanos.

______ 8. Gregorio es el esposo de la mamá de María.

______ 9. Clara es la hermanastra de José.

SCORE

Quiz 6-1

III. Writing

C. Identify and describe each member of this family. Include ages, likes and dislikes, pastimes, appearance, and personality. (12 points)

10. ____

____

11. ____

____

12. ____

____

SCORE ______

IV. Culture

D. Based on the information in your textbook, respond with **a) cierto** or **b) falso** to the following statements. (5 points)

__________ **13.** People in Spanish-speaking countries tend to spend more time with friends and family than do people in the United States.

__________ **14.** Godparents are expected to give advice, affection, and even help with school-related expenses.

SCORE ______

TOTAL SCORE ______ /35

CAPÍTULO 6

Nombre ______________________ Clase ____________ Fecha ____________

Entre familia

Quiz 6-2

SEGUNDO PASO

Maximum Score: 35

I. Listening

A. Pedro is describing several photos that he has found. Listen to his descriptions and see if you can match each photo with what he says. (10 points)

a.

b.

c.

d.

e.

1. ______ 2. ______ 3. ______ 4. ______ 5. ______

SCORE

II. Reading

B. Read each of the following descriptions below and decide which picture it best matches. More than one description may match each photo. (10 points)

a.

b.

c.

______ 6. Quiero mucho a mis hijas, pero Susana es un poco traviesa.

______ 7. A veces salgo con mi mamá y mi hermana mayor a cenar en un restaurante mexicano. ¡Qué divertido!

Quiz 6-2

_____ **8.** Mi papá y yo casi siempre visitamos a mi abuelita los fines de semana. Ella es muy cariñosa. Tiene canas y los ojos de color café.

_____ **9.** Mi papá es un poco gordo. ¿Y mi hermana mayor Sara? Pues, ella es muy inteligente y lista. Mañana hacemos una fiesta para celebrar su graduación del colegio.

_____ **10.** Tengo 69 años, pero nunca estoy aburrida porque mi hijo y mi nieto me visitan casi todos los fines de semana. Y durante el verano siempre hacemos un viaje juntos.

SCORE ____

III. Writing

C. You're planning to stay with a family in Guatemala next summer. Let them know your plans by writing a sentence in Spanish for each of the following pieces of information. (12 points)

11. You're leaving New York on June 15.

____

12. You are short, dark, and thin.

____

13. You want to visit your friend Rodolfo when you're in Guatemala.

____

14. You also want to visit some shopping malls.

____

SCORE ____

IV. Culture

D. Based on the information in your textbook, respond with **a) cierto** or **b) falso** to the statements below. (3 points)

_____ **15.** Spanish speakers often share their problems with other family members rather than dealing with them alone.

_____ **16.** In Spanish-speaking families, the desire to be alone for long periods might be interpreted as a sign of a problem.

_____ **17.** Teenagers in Spain and Latin America rarely help out around the house.

SCORE ____

TOTAL SCORE ____ /35

CAPÍTULO 6

Nombre ______________________ Clase ____________ Fecha ____________

Entre familia

Quiz 6-3

TERCER PASO

Maximum Score: 30

I. Listening

A. María Elena is describing the chores that her family must do to keep the house neat and clean. Based on María Elena's description, put items **a** to **e** in the order they happen. (10 points)

a.

b.

c.

d.

e.

1. _____ 2. _____ 3. _____ 4. _____ 5. _____

SCORE [ ]

II. Reading

B. Read the following letter from an advice column. Then indicate with **sí** or **no** whether the letter writer should take the advice that follows. (8 points)

Querida Ana,

Tengo un problema. Mi mamá dice que no ayudo lo suficiente en casa. Dice que siempre miro mucha televisión. Pero no es cierto. Mi mamá no comprende. Cuando regreso del colegio todos los días, quiero descansar un poco. Mis clases este semestre son difíciles y siempre tengo mucha tarea. No es posible hacer la tarea y ayudar a mi mamá. ¿Qué debo hacer?

Un buen estudiante con problemas en casa

"Buen estudiante"...

_____ 6. debe hablar con su mamá y explicar (*explain*) la situación.

_____ 7. debe salir con sus amigos después de clases porque la tarea no es importante.

Quiz 6-3

______ **8.** debe ayudar a su mamá los fines de semana cuando no tiene tarea.

______ **9.** no debe ayudar a su mamá ni hacer la tarea.

SCORE

III. Writing

C. Rogelio is taking care of his younger brothers and sisters today. One of his brothers is asking who should do which household chores. Using the cues in parentheses, write Rogelio's answers in Spanish. (12 points)

10. The cat needs attention. Who should look after it? (You should . . .)

____

11. The living room is a mess. Should Marta or Ramón clean it? (She should . . .)

____

12. Everyone is ready to eat. Shouldn't you and I set the table? (We should . . .)

____

13. Maribel and Rubén are just goofing around. Shouldn't they clean the kitchen? (They should . . .)

____

14. The grass is really tall. Who should cut it? (I should . . .)

____

15. The clothes you just washed are all wrinkled. Should Marisol and I iron them? (You (both) should . . .)

____

SCORE

TOTAL SCORE /30

CUMULATIVE SCORE FOR QUIZZES 1–3 /100

Nombre ______________________________ Clase ____________ Fecha ____________

Entre familia

Chapter 6 Test

I. Listening

Maximum Score: 30 points

A. Look carefully at Ana's family tree and listen as she introduces her family to you. Match the correct name to each family member she introduces. (15 points)

a. Olga Pérez Gómez de Rivera
b. Eduardo Rivera Pérez
c. Jorge Rivera Pérez
d. Elsa Acosta de Pérez
e. Luisa Gómez de Pérez

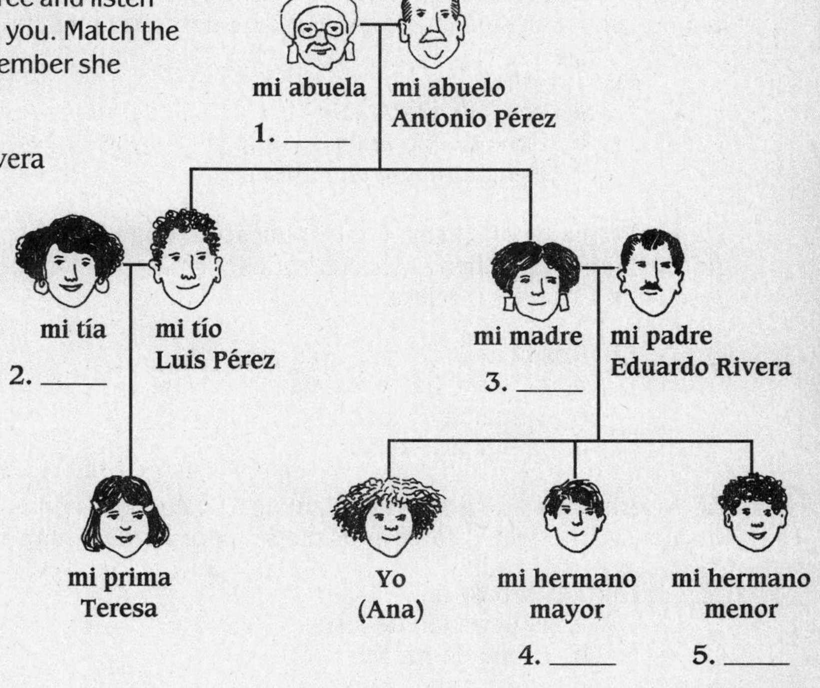

SCORE

B. Listen to a few short dialogues at the Pérez house. Decide which picture goes with each dialogue. Then decide if the statement in item 10 is **a) true** or **b) false**. (15 points)

a.

b.

c.

d.

6. ______ 7. ______ 8. ______ 9. ______

10. ______ The children complain a lot about doing chores.

SCORE

CAPÍTULO 6

Nombre ______________________ Clase ______________ Fecha ______________

Chapter 6 Test

II. Reading

Maximum Score: 30 points

C. Read the description that José gives about his extended family. Write the letter of the phrase that best completes his description. (15 points)

Nuestra familia es bastante grande y muy divertida. Tengo dos hermanas y dos hermanos. Mi mamá se llama Rebeca y tiene dos hermanos, mi tía Alicia y mi tío Arturo.

_____ **11.** Tía Alicia...
- **a.** es la tía de Rafael
- **b.** tiene treinta años
- **c.** es la hermana de Rebeca

Tía Alicia es alta y pelirroja y muy simpática. Ella es profesora de español en un colegio. Su hijo, Rafael, tiene dieciocho años y es estudiante. Su hija, mi prima Rosita, tiene doce años y es muy traviesa.

_____ **12.** Rosita es...
- **a.** la hermana de Rafael
- **b.** la mamá de José
- **c.** la hija de Arturo

Tío Arturo y Tía Luisa viven en Santiago y tienen tres hijas que se llaman Marta, Sara y Susana. Marta tiene catorce años. Es un poco gorda y muy simpática.

_____ **13.** Tío Arturo es...
- **a.** el hermano de José
- **b.** primo de Rafael
- **c.** el esposo de Luisa

Sara tiene trece años. Susana, la hija menor, tiene sólo tres años. Todas son muy inteligentes. Mis abuelos, Elsa y Manuel, viven muy cerca de aquí. Nos gusta salir con ellos y con nuestros tíos y primos. Mi abuelo es trabajador y debe descansar más. Elsa dice que debe ayudar más en casa.

_____ **14.** Elsa es...
- **a.** la mamá de Pilar
- **b.** la tía de José
- **c.** la abuela de José

Chapter 6 Test

Papá se llama Rogelio y mis padres tienen otros cuatro hijos—dos hijos y dos hijas. Mis hermanas son Pilar y Juanita. Tomás y Julio son mis hermanos. ¡Qué buena familia!

_____ **15.** Tomás es...
- **a.** el papá de Rosita
- **b.** el hermano de José
- **c.** el abuelo de Rebeca

SCORE ____

D. Norma does a lot on weekends. For each blank, write the letter of the word that best completes her description. (15 points)

16. Los sábados, ayudo mucho en casa. Por la mañana siempre _____ la cama.
- **a.** pongo
- **b.** hago
- **c.** salgo

17. También _____ la mesa para el almuerzo. Y a veces limpio la piscina.
- **a.** pone
- **b.** pones
- **c.** pongo

18. Por la tarde _____ con mis amigos a un café o restaurante.
- **a.** salgo
- **b.** salimos
- **c.** ponemos

19. Por la noche _____ familia siempre hace algo.
- **a.** nuestro
- **b.** nuestra
- **c.** su

20. Los domingos, mis padres y yo siempre visitamos _____ mis abuelos y salimos a cenar. ¡Es una familia muy unida!
- **a.** a
- **b.** (no word needed)
- **c.** con

SCORE ____

Nombre ______________________ Clase ____________ Fecha ____________

Chapter 6 Test

III. Culture

Maximum Score: 12 points

E. Read the statements below. Based on the information in your textbook, determine whether the statements are **a) cierto** or **b) falso**. (6 points)

_____ 21. In Spanish-speaking countries, families are often large and close-knit.

_____ 22. Family members in Spanish-speaking countries rarely spend time together or depend on each other for support.

SCORE

CAPÍTULO 6

F. Explain two roles and responsibilities of godparents in Hispanic culture. (6 points)

23. ____

____

24. ____

____

SCORE

IV. Writing

Maximum Score: 28 points

G. Imagine you're a member of the Gómez family. You are showing this portrait of your family to a friend. Choose five people and write two sentences to introduce and describe each of them. Each sentence should include two physical descriptions. (15 points)

25. ______________________________

____

26. ______________________________

____

27. ______________________________

____

28. ______________________________

____

29. ______________________________

____

SCORE ______

Chapter 6 Test

H. It was your job to clean the house today, but you didn't have time. You left a lot of chores to be done. Your younger brother agreed to help you out, but he needs to know what to do. Based on the picture, write a note telling your brother what he ought to do to help you. Your note should include at least three sentences and at least five things your brother should do. (13 points)

30. ____

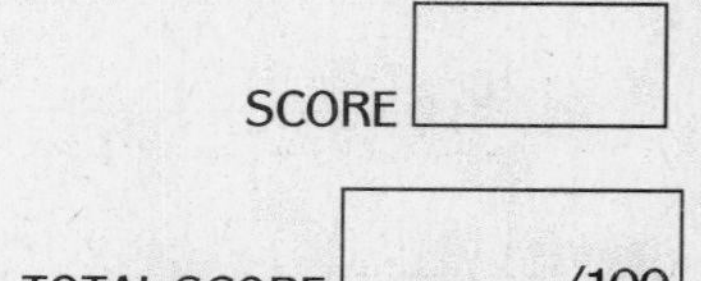

SCORE

TOTAL SCORE /100

CAPÍTULO 6 Chapter Test Score Sheet

Circle the letter that matches the most appropriate response.

I. Listening

Maximum Score: 30 points

A. (15 points)

1. a b c d e
2. a b c d e
3. a b c d e
4. a b c d e
5. a b c d e

SCORE ☐

B. (15 points)

6. a b c d e
7. a b c d e
8. a b c d e
9. a b c d e
10. a b

SCORE ☐

II. Reading

Maximum Score: 30 points

C. (15 points)

11. a b c d
12. a b c d
13. a b c d
14. a b c d
15. a b c d

SCORE ☐

D. (15 points)

16. a b c
17. a b c
18. a b c
19. a b c
20. a b c

SCORE ☐

III. Culture

Maximum Score: 12 points

E. (6 points)

21. a b
22. a b

SCORE ☐

F. (6 points)

23. ______________________________
____
24. ______________________________
____

SCORE ☐

Nombre ______________________ Clase ____________ Fecha ____________

CAPÍTULO 6

IV. Writing

Maximum Score: 28 points

G. (15 points)

25. ____________________

26. ____________________

27. ____________________

28. ____________________

29. ____________________

SCORE

H. (13 points)

30. ____________________

SCORE

TOTAL SCORE /100

RESOURCES

Scripts and Answers

CAPÍTULO 6

Additional Listening Activity 6-1, p. 69

SUSANA ¡Hola! Me llamo Susana Pérez. Tengo catorce años. Voy a describirles a mi familia. Primero, tengo dos hermanos. Mi hermano menor se llama Cristián y tiene doce años. Mi hermana mayor se llama Lucía y tiene quince años. Mis padres se llaman Jorge y Consuelo. Mi padre tiene cuarenta años. Mi mamá tiene treinta y siete años. Mi abuelo se llama Alberto y tiene setenta y seis años. Rosa, mi abuelita, tiene setenta y dos años. Mi tío Antonio es el hermano menor de mi mamá. Tiene treinta y cinco años. Su esposa, mi tía Ana, tiene treinta y seis años. Mis dos primos, Carmen y Alfonso, son muy simpáticos y divertidos y me gusta visitar con ellos. Ella tiene catorce años y mi primo Alfonso tiene dieciséis años.

Additional Listening Activity 6-2, p. 69

LUISA Tengo una familia bastante grande, pero unida. Somos seis en casa. Tengo tres hermanos mayores, Ramón, Adán y César. Hacemos mucho juntos. Una de mis cosas favoritas es visitar a mis abuelos. Viven muy cerca de nosotros y tienen dos gatos. Cada domingo vamos a su casa para pasar el día. Mi abuela siempre nos prepara una cena riquísima.

Additional Listening Activity 6-3, p. 70

PEDRO Pues, ¿qué hacemos nosotros los fines de semana? Eh... muchas cosas, claro, pero casi siempre vamos los domingos a un restaurante para cenar. A mi mamá le gusta salir a cenar. Y tú, Alicia, ¿qué hacen ustedes juntos los fines de semana?

ALICIA A nosotros nos gusta salir de la casa a pasar el día en el parque. Es muy divertido jugar al fútbol afuera con mis hermanos.

ESTEBAN Como ustedes ya saben, a mí me encanta nadar. Lo bueno es que mis tíos viven muy cerca de la playa y los visitamos cada fin de semana y lo pasamos muy bien con ellos.

PAULA Pues tengo que decirles que no hacemos nada los fines de semana. Después de pasar una semana tan ocupada, no queremos salir. Por eso, nos quedamos en casa y miramos la televisión juntos.

Additional Listening Activity 6-4, p. 70

PATRICIA Oye, Tomás, ¿qué tal si vamos de compras este miércoles, después de clases?

TOMÁS ¿El miércoles? No, Patricia... es imposible. El miércoles salgo con Carlos. Vamos a visitar a Ernesto en el hospital. Pero vamos a las cuatro. ¿Quieres ir el miércoles más tarde, como a las seis?

PATRICIA No puedo. El miércoles salimos Isabel y yo. Vamos a ver esa película nueva.

TOMÁS Mmm... ¿y no podemos ir el lunes?

PATRICIA Pues, el lunes no salgo con nadie, pero tengo una cita con el dentista por la tarde. ¿Qué haces el jueves?

TOMÁS Creo que Teresa y yo vamos a ir a un concierto de guitarra.

PATRICIA Tomás, tenemos que encontrar algo para mamá. No quiero esperar hasta el sábado porque ya es muy tarde.

TOMÁS Bueno, ¿podemos ir el viernes?

PATRICIA Casi siempre los viernes salgo con Verónica, pero puedo cancelar esta vez. ¿Qué haces tú este viernes?

TOMÁS Nada en particular.

PATRICIA Muy bien. Vamos el viernes, entonces.

Additional Listening Activity 6-5, p. 71

NARRADOR Hoy es día de fiesta en casa de los Acosta. Esta noche la familia celebra el cumpleaños de la Sra. Acosta. Pero antes de la fiesta, doña Rebeca, la abuela, está en la cocina. Prepara la comida: empanadas, puerco asado, frijoles negros con arroz a la cubana—¡qué rico! El Sr. Acosta está afuera. Lava el carro de su esposa. En el comedor, Anita, la hija menor de los Acosta, pone la mesa. Tomás, el hijo mayor de los Acosta, está en la sala. Pasa la aspiradora. Todo tiene que estar muy limpio porque van a venir muchos invitados.

Additional Listening Activity 6-6, p. 71

TIO RICARDO Queridos sobrinos. Sus padres van a salir todos los días y yo trabajo hasta muy tarde. Uds. deben ayudarnos más en los quehaceres de la casa. Tú, Fernando, debes lavar los platos todos los días y tú, Ana, debes poner la mesa antes de que lleguen tus padres para la cena. Tú, Luisa, debes pasar la aspiradora y Gloria debe hacer las camas. Leticia debe limpiar los cuartos y tú, Simón, debes lavar el carro. Tu amigo Antonio puede ayudarte. Gabriela debe cuidar a su hermanito Pepe en las tardes y Javier debe trabajar en el jardín para mantenerlo limpio. ¡No hay nada más bonito que una familia unida!, ¿verdad?

Answers to Additional Listening Activities

Additional Listening Activity 6-1, p. 69

Los abuelos: Alberto, 76 años; Rosa, 72 años
Los padres: Jorge, 40 años; Consuelo, 37 años
Los tíos: Antonio, 35 años; Ana, 36 años
Los hermanos: Cristián, 12 años; Lucía, 15 años
Los primos: Carmen, 14 años; Alfonso, 16 años

Additional Listening Activity 6-2, p. 69

1. a
2. b
3. a
4. a

Additional Listening Activity 6-3, p. 70

1. Pedro: No matching picture.
2. Alicia: c
3. Esteban: a
4. Paula: b

Additional Listening Activity 6-4, p. 70

They can go shopping together on Friday.

Additional Listening Activity 6-5, p. 71

1. Doña Rébeca: prepara la comida
2. Sr. Acosta: lava el carro
3. Anita: pone la mesa
4. Tomás: pasa la aspiradora

Additional Listening Activity 6-6, p. 71

lavar los platos: Fernando
poner la mesa: Ana
hacer la cama: Gloria
limpiar el cuarto: Leticia
pasar la aspiradora: Luisa
lavar el carro: Simón
cuidar al hermanito: Gabriela
trabajar en el jardín: Javier

Listening Scripts for Quizzes

Quiz 6-1 Capítulo 6 Primer paso

I. Listening

A.
1. Juana es mi tía.
2. Pilar es la hermana de José.
3. Rosa es mi abuela.
4. Julia y Elena son mis primas.
5. Juana es la abuela de Pedro.

Quiz 6-2 Capítulo 6 Segundo paso

I. Listening

A.
1. A veces son muy traviesos. Uno de ellos es delgado y el otro es gordo.
2. Tiene ochenta años pero se ve joven. Tiene los ojos azules y el pelo blanco.
3. Son personas muy especiales. Uno es alto y pelirrojo. Una es baja y un poco gorda.
4. Es delgado y tiene los ojos de color café con pelo negro.
5. Esta chica es pelirroja con ojos azules y es bastante delgada.

Quiz 6-3 Capítulo 6 Tercer paso

I. Listening

A. En mi casa hay mucho que hacer y todos ayudamos a mamá. Primero hago la cama y después paso la aspiradora. Mi mamá prepara el desayuno para nosotros y comemos juntos. Después del desayuno, mi papá limpia la cocina y luego mi hermano Pedro saca la basura. Por la tarde, mi hermana Juana trabaja con mamá en el jardín. Después de todo eso, la casa está en orden y todos descansamos un rato.

ANSWERS Quiz 6-1

I. Listening

A. (10 points: 2 points per item)
1. sí
2. no
3. no
4. sí
5. no

II. Reading

B. (8 points: 2 points per item)
6. sí
7. no
8. sí
9. sí

III. Writing

C. (12 points: 4 points per item)
Answers will vary. Possible answers:
10. Pilar es morena y baja. A ella le gusta escuchar música.
11. Jamie toca bien el piano. Es muy artístico.
12. Santiago es guapo y cómico. A él le gusta leer el periódico.

IV. Culture

D. (5 points: 2 1/2 points per item)
13. a
14. a

ANSWERS Quiz 6-2

I. Listening

A. (10 points: 2 points per item)
1. c
2. a
3. b
4. d
5. e

II. Reading

B. (10 points: 2 points per item)
6. c
7. a
8. b
9. c
10. b

III. Writing

C. (12 points: 3 points per item)
11. Salgo de Nueva York el quince de junio.
12. Soy bajo/a, moreno/a y delgado/a.
13. Quiero visitar a mi amigo Rodolfo cuando estoy en Guatemala.
14. Quiero visitar unos centros comerciales también.

IV. Culture

D. (3 points: 1 point per item)
15. a
16. a
17. b

ANSWERS Quiz 6-3

I. Listening

A. (10 points: 2 points per item)
1. d
2. b
3. c
4. e
5. a

II. Reading

B. (8 points: 2 points per item)
6. sí
7. no
8. sí
9. no

III. Writing

C. (12 points: 2 points per items)
10. Tú debes cuidar al gato.
11. Ella debe limpiar la sala.
12. Nosotros debemos poner la mesa.
13. Ellos deben limpiar la cocina.
14. Yo debo cortar el césped.
15. Ustedes deben planchar la ropa.

Scripts for Chapter Test Capítulo 6

I. Listening

A. Hola, me llamo Ana. Vivo en la ciudad de Concepción, Chile. Quiero presentarles a mi familia. Primero, a mi mamá. Se llama Olga. Es muy cariñosa y amable. Mi padre se llama Eduardo. Es cariñoso también pero un poco estricto. Mi tía Elsa y mi tío Luis viven en Valparaíso. Son muy simpáticos. Me gusta mucho visitarlos. Tienen una hija, mi prima Teresa. Mis abuelos viven en Valparaíso también. Mi abuela se llama Luisa Gómez de Pérez. Son muy cariñosos. Son viejos pero se ven muy jóvenes. Mi hermano mayor es Jorge. Es muy inteligente. Asiste a la universidad. Mi hermano menor se llama Eduardo. Lo quiero mucho, pero es un poco travieso. Bueno, ésta es mi familia. Somos todos muy unidos.

B. **6.** — ¿Qué debes hacer en casa hoy?
— Debo cuidar al gato.

7. — ¿Qué hago para ayudar, papá?
— ¿Por qué no cortas el césped?

8. — ¿Pones la mesa hoy, Juan?
— Sí, papá. Pongo la mesa todos los lunes.

9. — A mi hermana María le gusta pasar la aspiradora.
— Sí, me gusta porque soy muy organizada.

Answers to Chapter Test

I. Listening Maximum Score: 30 points

A. (15 points: 3 points per item)
1. e
2. d
3. a
4. c
5. b

B. (15 points: 3 points per item)
6. c
7. a
8. b
9. d
10. b

II. Reading Maximum Score: 30 points

C. (15 points: 3 points per item)
11. d
12. a
13. c
14. c
15. b

D. (15 points: 3 points per item)
16. b
17. c
18. a
19. b
20. a

III. Culture Maximum Score: 12 points

E. (6 points: 3 points per item)
21. a
22. b

F. (6 points: 3 points per item)
23. and **24.** Answers will vary but should include: life-long relationship, provide affection, advice, occasional support with school or careers. Having godparents increases the extended family.

IV. Writing Maximum Score: 28 points

G. (15 points: 3 points per item)
Answers will vary. Possible answers:
25. Éste es mi padre. Es muy alto y muy cómico.
26. Ésta es mi mamá. Es muy cariñosa y muy bonita.
27. Éste es mi hermano menor. Es muy divertido y un poco travieso.
28. Ésta es mi hermana menor. Es muy pequeña y muy bonita.
29. Éste es mi hermano mayor. Es muy inteligente y delgado.

H. (13 points)
Answers will vary. Possible answer:
30. Hay muchas cosas que hacer y necesito tu ayuda. Debes cuidar al gato, limpiar la mesa y lavar la ropa. También debes planchar la ropa, pasar la aspiradora y hacer la cama. Gracias, hermano.

Entre familia

DE ANTEMANO

1 When Raquel shows Armando her family's photo album, he asks some questions about her family. Can you match Armando's questions with Raquel's answers?

b 1. ¿De dónde es tu tía Luisa?

e 2. ¿Dónde vive tu hermano Carlos ahora?

d 3. A Uds. les gusta la música, ¿verdad?

a 4. ¿Qué hacen Uds. durante las vacaciones de Navidad?

c 5. ¿Sales mucho con tus hermanos?

a. Para Navidades, vamos a Tampa y visitamos a mis tíos y mis abuelos que viven allí.

b. Ella es de Cuba, como mis padres.

c. Sí, salgo con ellos bastante. Muchas veces voy con mis hermanos al cine o al centro comercial. ¡A veces salimos a bailar!

d. ¡Muchísimo! Todos tocamos por lo menos un instrumento musical.

e. Ahora él vive en Gainesville. Estudia en la Universidad de Florida.

2 Look at the family portraits and circle the description that best matches each portrait.

1\.

a. Ésta es mi familia: mis padres, mi hermano, mi hermana y mi abuela.
(b.) Aquí estamos todos: mi madre, mi padre, mi hermano y yo.
c. Aquí ves a mi familia: mi padre, mi madre, mi hermana, nuestro perro y yo.

2\.

a. Éstos son mis hermanos.
b. En esta foto estamos todos: mi padre, mi madre y yo.
(c.) Éstos son mis abuelos.

3\.

a. Éstos son mis padres.
(b.) Ésta es mi familia: mis padres, mis dos hermanos menores y yo.
c. Ésta es mi familia: mis padres, mis dos primos y mi abuelo.

Practice and Activity Book p. 61

PRIMER PASO

3 Look over the **Vocabulario** on p. 153 of your textbook, then complete the crossword puzzle.

Horizontales

5. El padre de tu padre
8. El hijo de tu madre y tu padrastro
10. Lo contrario de hermano
12. La hermana de tu padre
13. Los hijos de tu tío
14. La madre de tu padre
15. Las hijas de tus tíos

Verticales

1. El hermano de tu madre
2. Lo contrario de padre
3. La hija de tu madrastra o tu padrastro
4. Lo contrario de esposa
6. El hijo de tu abuelo y el esposo de tu madre
7. El esposo de tu madre, pero que no es tu verdadero padre
9. La esposa de tu padre, pero que no es tu verdadera madre
10. Tu padre es el ___ de tu abuela paterna
11. Tu madre es la ___ de tu abuelo materno

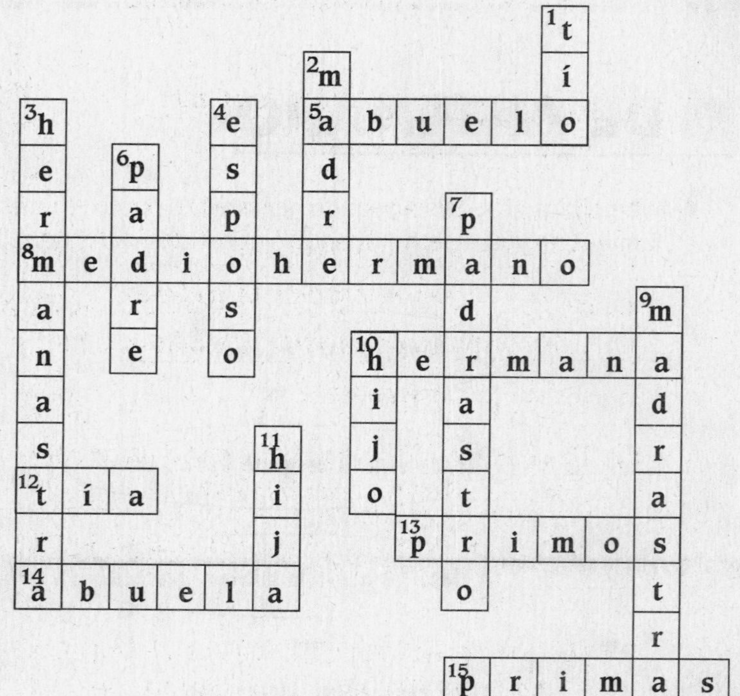

4 Guillermo Montes has invited Lupe to his house for a family party. She's never met any of his family before, and as his relatives come into the living room, Guillermo points out everyone to Lupe. Complete his sentences with **éste**, **ésta**, **éstos**, or **éstas**.

1. ___Éstas___ son mis primas, Rosita y Carmen. Son estudiantes en la Universidad de Florida. Y 2. ___ésta___ es mi abuelita. Ella vive con nosotros. 3. ___Éstos___ son mis hermanitos, Alfonso y Carlitos. Son super-pesados (*pains*). 4. ___Ésta___ es mi madre. A ella le gustan mucho estas fiestas grandes. 5. ___Éstos___ son mis tíos, Isabel y Armando. Ellos viven en Orlando. 6. ___Ésta___ es mi hermana mayor, Gloria... ¡ y 7. ___éste___ es mi sobrinito, Javier! Sólo tiene seis meses, pero ya sé que es muy inteligente. Y 8. ___éste___ es mi padre. A él le gustan las fiestas, pero prefiere (*he prefers*) leer el periódico.

Practice and Activity Book p. 62

5 Imagine that you're having a conversation with Pilar Guzmán Franco about her family. Using her family tree and the cues provided, write your questions and Pilar's answers.

1. TÚ (Ask how many people there are in Pilar's family.)
   ¿Cuántas personas hay en tu familia?
2. PILAR **Hay once personas en mi familia./Somos once.**
3. TÚ (Ask what Pilar's parents are like.)
   ¿Cómo son tus padres?
4. PILAR **Possible answers: Mi padre es alto y tiene cincuenta años. Mi madre es estricta pero simpática.**
5. TÚ (Ask what Pilar's grandparents' names are.)
   ¿Cómo se llaman tus abuelos?
6. PILAR **Mi abuela se llama María y mi abuelo se llama Francisco.**
7. TÚ (Ask if Pilar and her brother have any pets **[animales domésticos]**.)
   ¿Tienen ustedes animales domésticos?
8. PILAR **Sí, tenemos un pez que se llama Tiburón y un perro que se llama Simba.**

6 The words **su** and **sus** can be confusing, because they mean so many different things: *your, his, her, their*. In a conversation, though, context will make the meaning of these words clear. How many meanings can the expressions below have? Circle all of the English expressions that match each Spanish one. Some expressions may have more than one match.

MODELO su hijo
(a.) el hijo de él **b.** los hijos de ella (c.) el hijo de Uds.

1. su casa
   (a.) la casa de ella (b.) la casa de Uds. **c.** las casas de Ud.
2. sus abuelos
   a. la abuela de ellos (b.) los abuelos de Ud. (c.) los abuelos de Uds.
3. su hermano
   (a.) el hermano de él **b.** los hermanos de ellos (c.) el hermano de Uds.
4. su madrastra
   a. la madrastra de nosotros (b.) la madrastra de María (c.) la madrastra de Uds.
5. sus padres
   (a.) los padres de Uds. (b.) el padre de ellas **c.** los padres de nosotras
6. su familia
   (a.) la familia de Pedro y Juan (b.) la familia de Uds. (c.) la familia de Ud.
7. sus primos
   a. los primos de nosotros **b.** el primo de ellas (c.) los primos de Lupe
8. sus tíos
   (a.) los tíos de Pilar (b.) los tíos de ella (c.) los tíos de Uds.

Practice and Activity Book p. 63

7 Complete Carmen's description of her family with the corrrect possessive adjectives.

¡Hola! Me llamo Carmen Iriarte y soy de Nueva York. Te quiero describir a 1. **mi** *(my)* familia. 2. **Nuestra** *(Our)* familia es un poco complicada—somos muy internacionales. 3. **Mi** *(My)* madre se llama Ana y es de Argentina originalmente. Ahora vive aquí en Nueva York. 4. **Su** *(Her)* hermano Roberto vive aquí también. 5. **Su** *(His)* esposa es de Irlanda. Se llama Maureen. 6. **Sus** *(Their)* dos hijitos se llaman Brian y Sara. Me encanta ir a la casa de 7. **mis** *(my)* tíos Roberto y Maureen y jugar con 8. **mis** *(my)* dos sobrinitos. 9. **Sus** *(their)* videojuegos son super-divertidos.

10. **Mis** *(My)* padres están divorciados. 11. **Mi** *(My)* padre Antonio es español. Vive ahora en España con 12. **su** *(his)* segunda esposa, Marián. 13. **Su** *(their)* casa está en Sevilla. Marián es muy cariñosa. 14. **Su** *(Her)* hijo Alfonso es 15. **mi** *(my)* hermanastro. Somos muy buenos amigos. Él quiere aprender inglés. Entonces, el año que viene, Alfonso va a vivir en 16. **nuestro** *(our)* apartamento en Nueva York y estudiar aquí. ¡Y yo voy a Sevilla a vivir en 17. **su** *(his)* piso y estudiar en 18. **su** *(his)* colegio. Qué complicado, ¿verdad?

8 Juan and Daniela Barrón are brother and sister. The pictures below are of their family. Take the role of either Juan or Daniela. First think of a name for each member of the family, and label him or her accordingly (Juan and Daniela are already labeled for you.) Also say how he or she is related to you. Then write a short paragraph answering the following questions.

Daniela Juan

¿Cuántas personas hay en tu familia? ¿Cómo es tu familia? ¿Cuántas personas viven en tu casa? ¿Tienen un animal doméstico? ¿Quiénes son las personas en estas fotos?

Answers will vary.

Practice and Activity Book p. 64

SEGUNDO PASO

9 Look at the Guzmán family tree in Activity 5. Answer the following questions about members of Pilar's family, using the what you've learned in Chapter 6 as well as any other words you know. Use your imagination to describe them.

1. ¿Cómo es Humberto?¿De qué color es su pelo? ¿De qué color son sus ojos? ¿Cuántos años tiene?

   Humberto es muy listo. Tiene el pelo negro y los ojos de color café. Él tiene dieciséis años.

2. ¿Cómo es María? ¿De qué color es su pelo? ¿Cuántos años tiene?

   María es muy simpática. Tiene canas. Tiene setenta años, pero se ve joven.

3. ¿Cómo es la abuela de Pilar? ¿De qué color es su pelo? ¿Cuántos años tiene?

   Elena es muy cariñosa. Es pelirroja. Tiene sesenta y siete años.

4. ¿Cómo es Simba? ¿De qué color es su pelo?

   Simba es un poco travieso y muy cómico. Su pelo es de color café.

10 How would you describe your best friend? Think of someone you're close to, either a family member or a friend, and write five to six sentences describing that person. Use the adjectives on pp. 158 and 159 of your textbook, as well as any others you've learned. Below are some other words you can use. Many of them are cognates.

comprensivo (a) *understanding*	**chismoso (a)** *gossipy*	**tener...años**
honrado (a) *honest*	**(im) paciente** *(im)patient*	**vivir en...**
(in) maduro (a) *(im)mature*	**irresponsable** *irresponsible*	**le gusta...**
sincero (a) *sincere*	**valiente** *brave*	

Answers will vary.

PRACTICE AND ACTIVITY BOOK CAPÍTULO 6 · ANSWERS

11 Combine elements from the columns to write four original sentences telling how often these people do the activities listed. Use the "personal a" as appropriate.

MODELO **Mis padres no visitan a sus primos nunca.**

yo	llamar (a)	mis abuelos	nunca
mis padres	visitar (a)	un museo	siempre
el/la profesor(a)	querer conocer (a)	sus primos	con frecuencia

1. **Answers will vary.**
2.
3.
4.

12 Look over this page from Andrés Benavente's address book. Then, using the cues provided, ask him for some information about his family.

1. what his family is like
   ¿Cómo es tu familia?
2. what he and his family do together on weekends
   ¿Qué hacen Uds. los fines de semana?
3. where where the people in his family live
   ¿Dónde viven tus parientes?

Jacobo Benavente Dávila
C.P. #278
Arecibo 00613
PUERTO RICO

Ana María Benavente
P.O. Box 8733
University of Florida
Gainesville, FL 31559
(en Miami: 3225 Buena
Vista Avenue
Miami, FL 35921)

Benigno Benavente Rubio y
Alma Ybarra de Benavente
C/ Palomar 92, 3
San Juan 00231
PUERTO RICO

Martín Berenger
Carrer dels Angels, 47, 6A
Barcelona 54022
ESPAÑA

Lidia Calero
11 Cra. 5 #6-64 B
Cartagena
COLOMBIA

Alejandro Galdós Sobejano
C/ Arteaga 1483
Colonia Centro, Nuevo
Laredo
Tamaulipas MEXICO

Carolina Irizarri de la
Vega
C/ 15 de septiembre, 42
Metapán, Sta. Ana
EL SALVADOR

Néstor Muñoz Arévalo
Avda. 13, #59, 7B
Maracaibo VENEZUELA

Now write Andrés's answers to your questions. Mention at least two things in item 5. In item 6, write where Andrés would say at least four members of his family live, including himself. Use your imagination!

4. **Answers will vary.**
5.
6.

Practice and Activity Book p. 66

13 Mercedes and Laura are tennis partners and friends. Below are their calendars for the next week. Read them through, then answer the questions below. Do Mercedes and Laura have anything in common besides tennis?

MODELO ¿Cuándo sale Mercedes con su tía Julia? ¿Qué hacen?
Mercedes sale con su tía Julia el viernes a la una. Van al centro comercial.

EL HORARIO DE MERCEDES

lunes 16	martes 17	miércoles 18	jueves 19	viernes 20	sábado 21	domingo 22
Laura— tenis 4:00	Mamá— visitar al tío Rubén 3:30	Miguel— 5:00 biblioteca para el examen de historia	Laura— tenis 4:00	Tía Julia— 1:00, al centro comercial Mamá y papá— cumpleaños de Abuelo	Roberto— cine 4:30 ♥	Abuela— misa 10:30

EL HORARIO DE LAURA

lunes 16	martes 17	miércoles 18	jueves 19	viernes 20	sábado 21	domingo 22
Mercedes— tenis 4:00	Sara— Café Gijón, 3:30	Mamá— regalo para Papá, 3:30	Mercedes— tenis 4:00	Roberto— Restaurante La Góndola 8:00 ♡	Mamá y Papá— →	¡PLAYA!

1. ¿Qué hacen Laura y Mercedes los lunes y los jueves?
   Las dos chicas juegan al tenis a las 4:00 los lunes y los jueves.
2. ¿Con quién sale Mercedes el miércoles? ¿Adónde van y qué hacen?
   Ella sale con Miguel. Van a la biblioteca y estudian.
3. ¿Con quién sale Laura el martes? ¿Qué hacen las dos chicas?
   El martes Laura sale con su amiga Sara. Van al Café Gijón y toman un refresco.
4. ¿Cuándo sale Mercedes con su mamá? ¿Y cuándo sale Laura con su mamá?
   Sale con su mamá el martes. Laura sale con su mamá el miércoles.
5. ¿Qué hace Mercedes el viernes, y con quién sale?
   Ella va a la fiesta de cumpleaños para su abuelo el viernes. Sale con sus padres.
6. ¿Qué hace Laura este fin de semana?
   Este fin de semana Laura va a la playa con sus padres.
7. ¿Cuándo sale Mercedes con su abuela? ¿Qué hacen?
   Ella sale con su abuela el domingo. Van a misa a las 10:30.
8. ¿Con quién sale Laura el viernes? ¿Y con quién sale Mercedes el sábado?
   Laura sale con Roberto el viernes a las 8:00. Mercedes sale con Roberto el sábado a las 4:30.

Practice and Activity Book p. 67

TERCER PASO

14 Match each of the problems pictured below with the most logical solution. Can you think of another solution to each problem?

1. h

2. d

3. f

4. g

5. a

6. b

7. e

8. c

Soluciones

a. Debes comprar una bicicleta nueva.
b. Debes estudiar mucho antes de los exámenes finales.
c. Debes dormir *(sleep)* ahora y hacer la tarea mañana.
d. No debes ir al cine si no tienes dinero.
e. Debes caminar con el perrito por la mañana, por la tarde y por la noche.
f. No debes tomar mucho sol en la playa.
g. Debes ir al restaurante a comer algo.
h. Debes organizar tu cuarto.

15 For each party listed below, write two sentences: one stating a problem that person or group has, and another stating what the party should do or should not do. Explain your solutions to the problems as in the **modelo**.

MODELO Nuestro colegio...
Nuestro colegio debe comprar un televisor para la cafetería porque me gusta ver televisión cuando como.

1. El profesor/La profesora de español... **debe...** ______

______

2. Mis amigos... **deben...** ______

______

3. Yo... **debo...** ______

______

Practice and Activity Book p. 68

4. Mis padres... **deben...**

5. Mi hermano/a... **debe...**

6. La clase de español... **debe...**

7. El director/La directora del colegio... **debe...**

16 On weekends, Irene and Merche like to get together and enjoy the free time. But sometimes it's hard to find free time, even on a Saturday morning. Follow the directions to create a phone conversation between Irene and Merche. **Answers will vary. Possible answers are:**

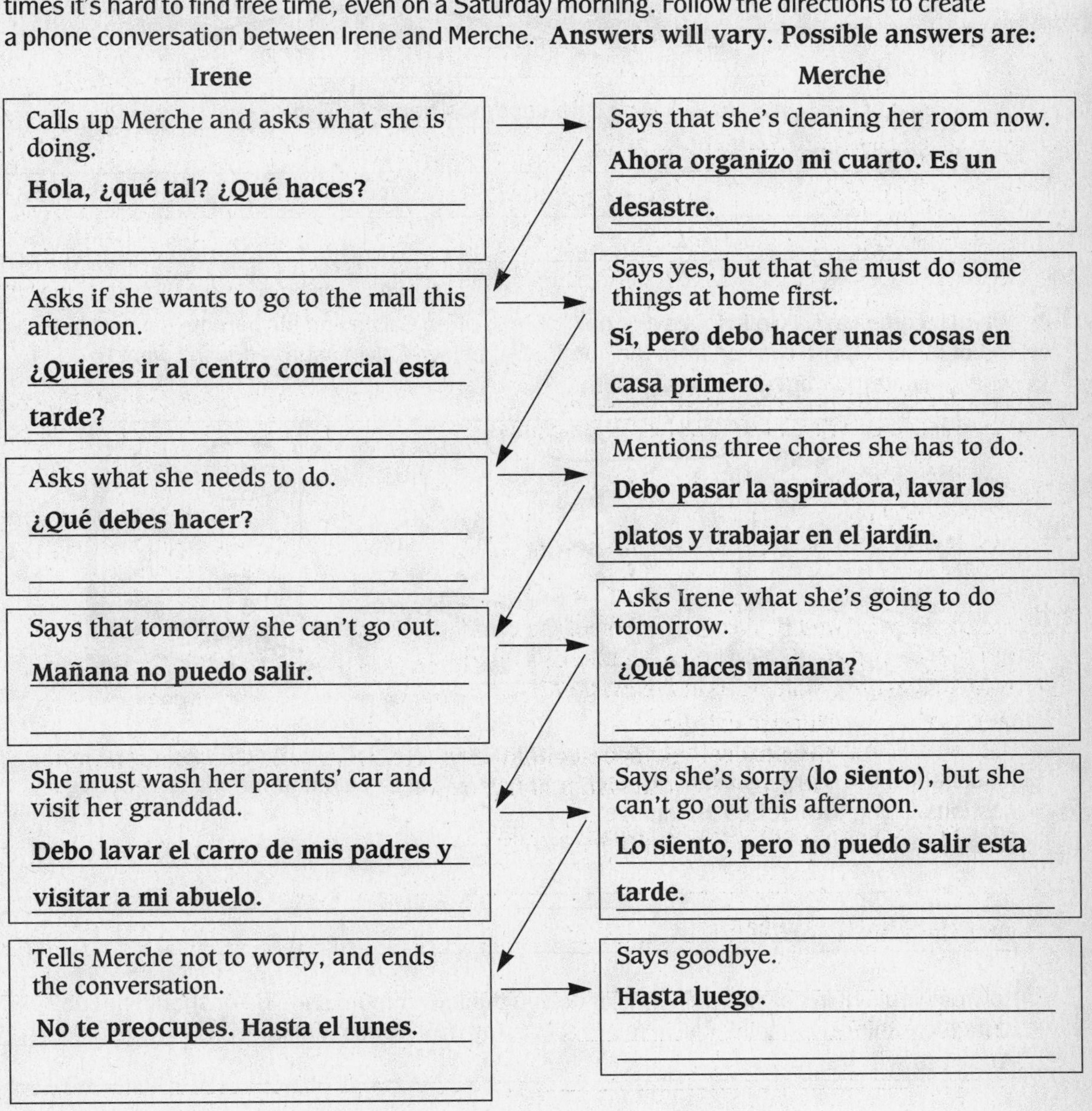

Irene	Merche
Calls up Merche and asks what she is doing. **Hola, ¿qué tal? ¿Qué haces?**	Says that she's cleaning her room now. **Ahora organizo mi cuarto. Es un desastre.**
Asks if she wants to go to the mall this afternoon. **¿Quieres ir al centro comercial esta tarde?**	Says yes, but that she must do some things at home first. **Sí, pero debo hacer unas cosas en casa primero.**
Asks what she needs to do. **¿Qué debes hacer?**	Mentions three chores she has to do. **Debo pasar la aspiradora, lavar los platos y trabajar en el jardín.**
Says that tomorrow she can't go out. **Mañana no puedo salir.**	Asks Irene what she's going to do tomorrow. **¿Qué haces mañana?**
She must wash her parents' car and visit her granddad. **Debo lavar el carro de mis padres y visitar a mi abuelo.**	Says she's sorry (**lo siento**), but she can't go out this afternoon. **Lo siento, pero no puedo salir esta tarde.**
Tells Merche not to worry, and ends the conversation. **No te preocupes. Hasta el lunes.**	Says goodbye. **Hasta luego.**

17 It's Saturday afternoon and Roberto and his friends Javier and Silvia are throwing a party tonight at Roberto's house. They've gathered to get the house into shape for the party, and there's a lot of work to do! Look at the picture of his house below. Then write the question Robert's friends would use to ask what they should do. Next put yourself in Roberto's place and write instructions telling each person what he or she should do. Split the work up evenly and make sure Roberto does his fair share, too.

Los amigos de Roberto preguntan: **¿Qué debemos hacer?**

Answers will vary.

18 When it comes to Calvin's duties and obligations, often Calvin and his parents have very different ideas. As you can see from the comic strip below, Calvin usually doesn't want to do what his parents want him to do.

Put yourself in the place of Calvin's mom, and imagine that you are trying to get him ready for school in the morning. What do you say to him? Write three recommendations or suggestions, using **(no) debes** + infinitive.

Answers will vary.

Now put yourself in Calvin's place. What do you think your mom should—or should not do? Write three things you think Calvin might say, using **(no) debes** + infinitive.

Answers will vary.

Practice and Activity Book p. 70

VAMOS A LEER

19 a. Below are three letters from the advice column in *Gente Joven*, a teen magazine. Read through the letters, using the reading strategies you've learned.

Querida *Gente Joven*,
Estoy desesperada y necesito su ayuda. Hay un chico en mi colegio que me gusta mucho. Se llama Francisco. Pero mis padres se oponen a° nuestra amistad°, porque piensan que es un muchacho "loco." Y ahora mis padres no me permiten hablar o salir con él. Pero quiero ser su amiga porque pienso que Francisco es una persona muy buena. ¿Qué debo hacer? **Cecilia**

se oponen a *are against, oppose*
amistad *friendship*

Querida *Gente Joven*,
Estoy preocupado por una amiga mía que se llama Elisa. Somos mejores amigos desde° el primer grado. Ahora Elisa está muy cambiada°. Ya no es la chica alegre, considerada, honesta, y trabajadora de antes. No estudia, no hace su tarea, no habla ni sale conmigo ni con sus otros amigos, siempre está cansada...su conducta no es la misma. Creo que tiene un problema muy grave, pero no sé qué hacer. **Diego**

desde *since*
cambiada *changed*

Querida *Gente Joven*,
Tengo 15 años y soy una chica responsable, madura e inteligente, pero mis padres son superestrictos conmigo. No me permiten usar el teléfono para llamar a mis amigos ni recibir llamadas°. No puedo salir durante la semana y sólo a veces los fines de semana. Mi vida es aburrida y triste. No sé por qué mis padres son así conmigo. Con mi hermano, no son tan estrictos. ¿Qué puedo hacer para ganar su confianza°? Gracias, **Amalia**

llamadas *phone calls*
confianza *confidence*

b. Answer the following questions.

1. What is the first letter about? A problem . . .
   a. at school (**b.**) with parents **c.** with a friend **d.** at work
2. What is the second letter about? A problem . . .
   a. with money **b.** with a brother/sister (**c.**) with a friend **d.** with parents
3. What is the third letter about? A problem . . .
   a. with a brother/sister **b.** with a teacher **c.** with a coach (**d.**) with parents
4. In the first letter, what do the parents think of Francisco? What does Cecilia think of him?
   The parents think Francisco is "crazy". Cecilia thinks he's a great person.
5. In the second letter, how is Elisa normally? And how has she been lately?
   Elisa is normally thoughtful, honest, hardworking, cheerful. Lately she's hasn't been studying or doing her homework, talking or going out with friends, and she's always tired.
6. In the third letter, how does Amalia describe herself? How does she compare her parents' treatment of her with the way her brother is treated?
   She says she is responsible, mature and intelligent. She says her parents aren't so strict with her brother.

c. You're a guest columnist for *Gente Joven*. Choose one letter to answer. Together, come up with at least three recommendations for solving the problem using **(no) debes** + infinitive.

Answers will vary.

Practice and Activity Book p. 71

CULTURA

20 As you read in the **Nota cultural** on p. 155 of your text, godparents are an important part of the Hispanic family. While the original function of godparents was to sponsor a child at its baptism and to take responsibility for its religious upbringing, today the **madrina** and **padrino** are also friends, advisors, and helpers to the child. They have very strong ties not only to their godchild, but also to the child's parents. The word **compadrazgo** literally means *joint paternity*. Mothers will refer to their child's godmother as **comadre** and fathers will call their child's godfather **compadre**, which also means *close friend*. Look over the greeting cards, and then work with a partner to answer the questions. Compare your answers with other classmates.

1. Can you figure out who the cards are for and what the occasion is?
   One is a birthday card for a godmother; the other is a card for a comadre.
2. Are cards for godparents generally found in card stores in the U.S.? Why or why not?
   Not typically, except in Spanish-speaking areas.
3. What does the fact that greeting cards exist especially for godparents tell you about their role in Spanish-speaking families?
   Godparents are as important as other family members; their birthdays are celebrated as other family members' birthdays are.
4. Why do you think that godparents play an important part in Hispanic family life?
   Spanish-speaking families often have a strong Catholic background in which baptism and religious training are important. Spanish-speaking cultures also place a high value on friendship, and close friends are often friends from childhood through adulthood. The relationships between godchild and godparent and parent and comadre/compadre reflect these cultural values.
5. Do you have godparents? What adults are close to and important to you?
   Answers will vary.

21 What kinds of generalizations can you make about privacy in the U.S. and in Spanish-speaking countries?
Answers will vary.

VAMOS A LEER

3 A los detalles

1. Un hombre sincero; arte; monte.
2. The student may answer any two of the following: un monte, un abanico de plumas, un puñal, un surtidor, un ciervo herido.
3. El arroyo.
4. *Answers will vary.*
5. *Answers will vary.*

4 Vamos a comprenderlo bien

1. Echar sus versos del alma (escribir poesía).
2. Sí.
3. Tiene mucha experiencia.
4. Una rosa blanca; También una rosa blanca; Answers will vary.

5 Reglas de acentuación: las palabras esdrújulas

1. antepenúltima
2. b
3. **océano** **América** **fáciles** **haciéndolo**
   imágenes **dámelo** **capítulo** **sílaba**
   auténticos **teléfono** **cámara** **vámonos**
   espíritu **énfasis** **llámame** **máquina**

6 Ortografía: las letras *r y rr*

1. Possible answers:

Palabras con una *r*	**Palabras con una *rr***
hombre	tierra
sincero	arroyo
versos	sierra
razón	arranca
pobres	
muera	
ramo	
corazón	
enero	
rosa	

2.

Palabra	**Regla**
ramo	iii
enero	i
honra	ii
sierra	i
rosa	iii

NATIVE SPEAKER ACTIVITY BOOK CAPÍTULO 6 · ANSWERS

VAMOS A ESCRIBIR

7 *Answers will vary.*

VAMOS A CONOCERNOS

8 A escuchar

Answers will vary.

9 A pensar

Answers will vary.

10 Así lo decimos nosotros

Palabra inglesa	Variante local	Español internacional
by chance	de chiripada	**por casualidad**
give someone a ride	dar un raite	llevar a alguien en carro
let's go	hórale	**vamos**
real good	**'ta padre**	estupendo
car	caracha	**carro**
I will fall	caidré	**caeré**
to kiss	pichionar	besar
truth	beldá	**verdad**
I will want	quedré	**querré**
brakes	brecas	**frenos**

VAMOS A CONVERSAR

11 *Answers will vary.*

¿Qué te gustaría hacer?

RESOURCES

¿Qué te gustaría hacer?

Chapter Teaching Resources Correlation Chart

RESOURCES	Print	Audiovisual
De antemano	*Practice and Activity Book*, p. 73	
	Video Guide OR *Videodisc Guide*	*Textbook Audiocassette 4A/Audio CD 7; Video Program* OR *Expanded Video Program, Videocassette 3* OR *Videodisc Program, Videodisc 4A*
Primer paso	*Chapter Teaching Resources, Book 2*	
	• Teaching Transparency Master 7-1, pp. 123, 126	*Teaching Transparency 7-1*
	• Additional Listening Activities 7-1, 7-2, p. 127 —Scripts, p. 154; Answers, p. 156	*Additional Listening Activities, Audiocassette 10A/Audio CD 7*
	• Realia 7-1, pp. 131, 133	
	• Situation Cards 7-1, pp. 134–135	
	• Student Response Forms, p. 136	
	• Quiz 7-1, pp. 139–140 —Scripts, p. 157; Answers, p. 158	*Assessment Items, Audiocassette 8A/Audio CD 7*
	Practice and Activity Book, pp. 74–76 —Answers: *Chapter Teaching Resources, Book 2*, pp. 162–164	
	Native Speaker Activity Book, pp. 26–30 —Answers: *Chapter Teaching Resources, Book 2*, pp. 173–174	
	Videodisc Guide	*Videodisc Program, Videodisc 4A*
Segundo paso	*Chapter Teaching Resources, Book 2*	
	• Communicative Activity 7-1, pp. 119–120	
	• Teaching Transparency Master 7-2, pp. 124, 126	*Teaching Transparency 7-2*
	• Additional Listening Activities 7-3, 7-4, p. 128 —Scripts, pp. 154–155; Answers, p. 156	*Additional Listening Activities, Audiocassette 10A/Audio CD 7*
	• Realia 7-2, pp. 132, 133	
	• Situation Cards 7-2, pp. 134–135	
	• Student Response Forms, p. 137	
	• Quiz 7-2, pp. 141–142 —Scripts, p. 157; Answers, p. 158	*Assessment Items, Audiocassette 8A/Audio CD 7*
	Practice and Activity Book, pp. 77–79 —Answers: *Chapter Teaching Resources, Book 2*, pp. 165–167	
	Native Speaker Activity Book, pp. 26–30 —Answers: *Chapter Teaching Resources, Book 2*, pp. 173–174	
	Videodisc Guide	*Videodisc Program, Videodisc 4A*
	Video Guide	*Video Program* OR *Expanded Video Program, Videocassette 3*
Tercer paso	*Chapter Teaching Resources, Book 2*	
	• Communicative Activity 7-2, pp. 121–122	
	• Teaching Transparency Master 7-3, pp. 125, 126	*Teaching Transparency 7-3*
	• Additional Listening Activities 7-5, 7-6, p. 129 —Scripts, p. 155; Answers, p. 156	*Additional Listening Activities, Audiocassette 10A/Audio CD 7*
	• Realia 7-2, pp. 132, 133	
	• Situation Cards 7-3, pp. 134–135	
	• Student Response Forms, p. 138	
	• Quiz 7-3, pp. 143–144 —Scripts, p. 157; Answers, p. 158	*Assessment Items, Audiocassette 8A/Audio CD 7*
	Practice and Activity Book, pp. 80–82 —Answers: *Chapter Teaching Resources, Book 2*, pp. 168–170	
	Native Speaker Activity Book, pp. 26–30 —Answers: *Chapter Teaching Resources, Book 2*, pp. 173–174	
	Videodisc Guide	*Videodisc Program, Videodisc 4A*

ASSESSMENT

Paso Quizzes
- *Chapter Teaching Resources, Book 2* Quizzes pp. 139–144 Scripts and answers pp. 157–158
- Assessment Items, *Audiocassette 8A/Audio CD 7*

Portfolio Assessment
- *Assessment Guide*, pp. 2–13, 20

Chapter Test
- *Chapter Teaching Resources, Book 2*, pp. 145–150 Test score sheets, pp. 151–152 Test scripts and answers, pp. 159–160
- *Assessment Guide*, Speaking Test, p. 31
- Assessment Items, *Audiocassette 8A/Audio CD 7*

Test Generator, Chapter 7

Communicative Activity 7-1 A

1. You're the switchboard operator at a hotel, in charge of taking messages for hotel guests. Your partner will call to talk to some people who are staying at your hotel. First answer the phone, then check your chart to see whether the guest your partner asks for is available or not. If the guest is out, first relay any message he or she may have left you, then take a message from the caller. Based on what the caller tells you, make a few notes in the message chart below.

MODELO — Diga.
— ¿Está la señorita Guadalupe Martínez?
— Un momento, a ver si está... No, lo siento, señor. No está.
— ¿Puedo dejar un recado?
— Sí, señor. ¿De parte de quién?
— Soy Juan Álvarez.
— ¿Cuál es el recado?
— Que si quiere ir al zoológico con nosotros mañana.

Huésped	Datos	Recado
Anita Jáquez Franco	no está en su habitación	
Santiago Fuentes Alarcón	en el restaurante	
Maricarmen Fernández	*línea ocupada*	
Carlos Unzueta Marcos	en la piscina	
Federico Montes	regresa a las diez	

2. You've got some friends who are in town for your brother's graduation. They're all staying at the same local hotel. Since you need to talk with your friends to make plans, call the hotel switchboard operator (your partner) and ask for each of them. If the switchboard operator says that the person you're asking for isn't there, then leave a message, using the notes below. (If there aren't any notes next to the person's name, just tell your partner that you'll call back later.)

Ana María Sánchez	*vamos al teatro mañana por la noche; ¿quiere ir también?*
Héctor Paredes	*la fiesta de graduación empieza a las diez*
Manuela Zamarripa	
Pedro Enríquez Castro	*ir a desayunar mañana; invito yo*
Margarita Cruz García	*¿está lista para ir?; ya venimos*

CAPÍTULO 7

Communicative Activity 7-1B

1. You've got some friends who are in town for your sister's wedding. They're all staying at the same local hotel. Since you need to talk with your friends to make plans, call the hotel switchboard operator (your partner) and ask for each of them. If the switchboard operator says that the person you're asking for isn't there, then leave a message using the notes below. (If there aren't any notes next to the person's name, just tell your partner that you'll call back later.)

MODELO — Diga.
— ¿Está la señorita Guadalupe Martínez?
— Un momento, a ver si está... No, lo siento, señor. No está.
— ¿Puedo dejar un recado?
— Sí, señor. ¿De parte de quién?
— Soy Juan Álvarez.
— ¿Cuál es el recado?
— Que si quiere ir al zoológico con nosotros mañana.

Anita Jáquez Franco	*la boda empieza a las tres*
Federico Montes	*venimos a las diez y media*
Santiago Fuentes Alarcón	*¿quiere desayunar conmigo mañana?*
Carlos Unzueta Marcos	
Maricarmen Fernández	*¿por qué siempre está ocupada la línea?*

CAPÍTULO 7

2. Now you're the switchboard operator, in charge of taking messages for hotel guests. You take messages for hotel guests. Your partner will call to talk to some people who are staying at your hotel. First answer the phone, then check your chart to see whether the guest your partner asks for is available or not. If the guest is out, first relay any message he or she may have left you, then take a message from the caller. Based on what the caller tells you, make a few notes in the message chart below.

Huésped	Datos	Recado
Margarita Cruz García	ya espera afuera	
Manuela Zamarripa	*línea ocupada*	
Ana María Sánchez	ya espera afuera	
Héctor Paredes	tiene que ducharse	
Pedro Enríquez Castro	no está	

Nombre ______________________ Clase ____________ Fecha ____________

Communicative Activity 7-2A

1. You want to get together and do something with a friend you haven't seen for a while. The only trouble is that both of you are very busy these days. You've found some free time during the week (Sunday, March 14 through Saturday, March 20) and you'd like to invite your friend to do something. Invite your friend to each event on the list below and don't stop until he or she accepts your invitation.

MODELO — ¿Te gustaría ir conmigo al museo de antropología el miércoles?
— ¿El miércoles? Lo siento, pero no puedo. Tengo que organizar mi cuarto.
— ¡Qué lástima! Y el jueves, ¿te gustaría ir al parque?

ir al campo el sábado por la tarde
ir a una fiesta el sábado por la noche
caminar en el parque
ir al teatro el jueves por la noche
ir al acuario el martes después de clases

2. Switch roles with your partner. It's Sunday evening, and a friend whom you haven't seen for a while has called to see if you'd like to do something together. For each thing your friend invites you to do, look at your datebook for the coming week to see whether you can go. If you can go, accept the invitation. If you can't, politely turn it down and explain why you can't go.

DIA Y FECHA	EVENTOS Y CITAS
domingo, 14 de marzo	¡Ay! ¡Estoy enfermo!
lunes, 15 de marzo	mucha tarea: composición de inglés
martes, 16 de marzo	tarea de química: leer el Capítulo 9
miércoles, 17 de marzo	partido de fútbol a las 6
jueves, 18 de marzo	ir al zoológico después de clases
viernes, 19 de marzo	¿mirar la televisión?
sábado, 20 de marzo	el museo con Marián por la tarde

Nombre ______________________ Clase ____________ Fecha ____________

Communicative Activity 7-2B

1. You want to get together and do something with a friend you haven't seen for a while. The only trouble is that both of you are very busy these days. It's Sunday evening, and a friend has called to see if you'd like to do something together. For each thing your friend invites you to do, look at your datebook for the coming week to see whether you can go. If you can go, accept the invitation. If you can't, politely turn it down and explain why you can't go.

MODELO — ¿Te gustaría ir conmigo al museo de antropología el miércoles?
— ¿El miércoles? Lo siento, pero no puedo. Tengo que organizar mi cuarto.
— ¡Qué lástima! Y el jueves, ¿te gustaría ir al parque?

DIA Y FECHA	EVENTOS Y CITAS
domingo, 14 de marzo	*¡qué día más aburrido!*
lunes, 15 de marzo	*biblioteca a las 7 con Marimar; geografía Capítulo 8*
martes, 16 de marzo	*piscina con Jorge, a las 4; tarea de inglés*
miércoles, 17 de marzo	
jueves, 18 de marzo	*estudiar para el examen de matemáticas*
viernes, 19 de marzo	*examen de matemáticas; fiesta de José Luis, a las 9*
sábado, 20 de marzo	*todo el día con los abuelos*

2. You've found some free time during the coming week (Sunday, March 14 through Saturday, March 20) and you'd like to invite your friend to do something. Invite your friend to each event on the list below and don't stop until he or she accepts your invitation.

ir al parque de atracciones esta noche
ir a una fiesta de cumpleaños el viernes a las nueve
ir a comer en un restaurante el miércoles a las seis
ir al cine el sábado por la tarde
ir al lago a nadar el domingo por la tarde

Nombre ______________________ Clase ______________ Fecha ______________

Teaching Transparency Master 7-1

CAPÍTULO 7

Nombre ______________________ Clase ____________ Fecha ____________

Teaching Transparency Master 7-2

CAPÍTULO 7

Nombre ______________________ Clase ______________ Fecha ____________

Teaching Transparency Master 7-3

CAPÍTULO 7

Using Teaching Transparencies 7-1, 7-2, 7-3

Teaching Transparency 7-1

1. **Speaking:** Review the functions targeted in Chapter 7 by asking students to give possible ways to answer the phone.
2. **Listening:** Read one or both of the conversations to the students and ask them to decide which picture it goes with.
   — **Diga.**
   — **Buenos días. Me gustaría hablar con el señor Tablada.**
   — **Un momento... Lo siento, señor/a, pero la línea está ocupada. ¿Le gustaría dejar un recado?**
   — **No gracias, llamo más tarde.**
   — **Muy bien.**

   — **Aló.**
   — **Hola Lorenzo, ¿qué tal?**
   — **Hola Marcos, ¿qué hay?**
   — **Oye, quiero saber si quieres ir conmigo al parque de atracciones este sábado.**
   — **Sí, cómo no.**
   — **Muy bien. Nos vemos entonces.**
3. **Pair work/Writing/Speaking:** Have students write a possible conversation between two people on the transparency in which one of them invites the other to a movie. Their conversation should include telephone-based greetings. Then have them role-play the conversation with a partner.

Teaching Transparency 7-2

1. **Speaking:** Ask students to figure out and tell you what the family might be getting ready to do.
2. **Listening:** Give each person on the transparency a name. Then ask students questions about who still needs to do what.
   — **¿Quién necesita afeitarse?**
   — **¿Necesita maquillarse mamá?**
   — **¿Qué necesita hacer la hija?**
3. **Speaking:** Have students talk about the things that they typically need to do before going out. For a challenge, give them the expression **tardar en** and ask them how long it takes them to do each thing.
   — **¿Cuánto tiempo tardas en ducharte?**
4. **Pair work/Speaking:** Have pairs of students create and then act out a short conversation between two people on the transparency. The conversation should include what each person still needs to do to get ready.

Teaching Transparency 7-3

1. **Listening:** Create a short conversation based on one of the scenes on the transparency and have students determine which scene it matches.
   — **¿Quieres ir al concierto conmigo?**
   — **No puedo. Estoy enferma.**
2. **Pair work/Speaking:** Have pairs of students create and then act out a possible conversation between two people in one of the four scenes. Their conversation should include an invitation, acceptance or refusal, and an excuse or explanation.
3. **Speaking:** Give each person in each scene a name. Then ask students what they think they are saying to each other.
4. **Writing:** Have students write a formal invitation to some upcoming event: a party, school dance, or concert, for example. Then have them exchange their invitations and either accept or decline in writing. If they decline, they should write the reason why.

PRIMER PASO

7-1 You will hear a series of statements made during phone conversations. As you listen, choose the most logical response to each statement that you hear.

1. **a.** Buenos días.
   b. Llamo más tarde.
2. **a.** Habla Fernando.
   b. ¿Puedo dejar un recado?
3. **a.** Está Germán, por favor?
   b. Soy yo, Teresa.
4. **a.** Sí. Dile que vamos al parque de atracciones mañana.
   b. Pronto.
5. **a.** Habla Raimundo Gómez.
   b. Bueno, llamo más tarde.
6. **a.** Hola. ¿Está Luisa, por favor?
   b. Gracias. Hasta luego.
7. **a.** De parte de Olivia Jiménez.
   b. Estoy bien, gracias. ¿Y Ud.?

7-2 The first person home at the Herrera household is responsible for listening to and taking down the messages left on the answering machine. Listen to each message and complete the missing information on the slips below.

Para: *todos*
De: ______
Teléfono: ______
Recado: *Quiere organizar...*
☐ Es urgente
☐ Va a llamar más tarde

1.

Para: ______
De: *Gonzalo Rayas*
Teléfono: ______
Recado: *Quiere ir...*
☐ Es urgente
☐ Va a llamar más tarde

2.

Para: *Verónica*
De: ______
Teléfono: ______
Recado: *Quiere estudiar para el examen de...*
☐ Es urgente
☐ Va a llamar más tarde

3.

CAPÍTULO 7

Additional Listening Activities

SEGUNDO PASO

7-3 Today is Friday, and Pepe is asking everyone about his or her plans for the weekend. Listen to the conversations. Write what each person plans to do next to his or her name.

1. Marisa: ______________________
2. Héctor: ______________________
3. Anita: ______________________
4. Sergio: ______________________
5. Lupe: ______________________

7-4 Everyone has something to do before leaving the house. Listen to each conversation and then choose the drawing that shows what each person needs to do.

1. Joaquín quiere __________ antes de ir al cine.

a. 
b. 

2. Aurelia necesita media hora para __________.

a. 
b. 

3. Carlos tiene que __________ antes de la fiesta.

a. 
b. 

4. Antes de salir, Víctor va a __________.

a. 
b. 

Nombre ______________ Clase __________ Fecha __________

TERCER PASO

7-5 Marcos is secretary of the Spanish Club this year and is in charge of calling club members to remind them about the class picnic. Listen to his conversations with some members and keep track of who's coming and who's not. If the person is not coming, write his or her excuse.

Nombre	Sí	No	Excusa
Elisa			
Cristóbal			
Marisol			
César			

7-6 When you're invited to do something that you don't want to do, you should politely turn the invitation down. Listen to the following invitations and choose the best refusal for each.

1. **a.** Gracias. Me gustaría ir, pero ya tengo planes.
   b. ¿La ópera? ¡Qué aburrido!
2. **a.** No, gracias. Tengo que trabajar esta tarde.
   b. No me gusta jugar a cartas.
3. **a.** Ahora no. Tengo prisa.
   b. Lo siento, pero tengo que hacer algo ahora mismo. Tal vez otro día.
4. **a.** Pues, gracias... pero no tengo ganas. Creo que estoy un poco enfermo/a.
   b. Si vas con Fernando, entonces no. Creo que es un chico muy antipático.
5. **a.** No, no me gustaría ir con Uds. al cine.
   b. No, gracias, no me gustan las películas.
6. **a.** No, quiero comer comida china. No me gusta.
   b. Me gustaría, pero esta noche no puedo. ¿Qué tal si vamos mañana a comer en el nuevo restaurante mexicano?

Additional Listening Activities

SONG

The nearly extinct **cóndor** (*condor*), with a wing span of as much as ten feet, is one of the largest birds in the world. It lives in the high Andes mountains of South America, and is the subject of many native legends. ***El cóndor pasa*** is probably the best-known Andean song in the world. The lyrics and this version of the song were written by Hernando Merino.

Andean music uses a wide array of unique stringed and wind instruments. Among them are **el charango** – a small, guitar-like instrument made from the shell of an armadillo, **la quena** – a kind of flute, **la zampoña** – an instrument similar to a set of pan pipes, and **el bombo** – a large drum.

El cóndor pasa

El cóndor, ave bella, pasará,
volará y jamás regresará.
¡Oh!
El indio en el desierto morirá,
Su corazón se elevará y volará.
¡Oh!
¿Quién sabe mañana adónde irán,
que harán, que comerán?
Quizás nunca más regresarán,
Y pienso que no viviré,
yo no podré.

This song is recorded on *Audio CD 7* and also on *Audiocassette 11: Songs*. Although it is presented in this chapter, it can be used at any time.

Nombre ______________________ Clase ____________ Fecha ____________

Mientras Ud. no estaba

Recado Telefónico

Para el/la Sr(a).

De parte de

De la compañía	Teléfono

Dijeron que

- ( ) le llamara Ud. al regresar
- ( ) llamaría más tarde

Recado:

Recibido por	Hora	Fecha

Realia 7-2

¡...porque no sería fiesta sin ti!

VAMOS A FESTEJAR A: ______________________

CON MOTIVO DE: ______________________

FECHA: ______________________

HORA: ______________________

DIRECCIÓN: ______________________

¡Te esperamos!

Junto con nuestros padres

Sres. Valero-Litri *Sres. Puig-Roca*

Tenemos el gusto de invitaros a nuestra boda,
que celebraremos el día 10 de mayo próximo,
en la Iglesia Ntra. Sra. de los Ángeles,
a las 6 de la tarde.

Miguel y Montserrat

Cena: Restaurante: La Piel del Oso *Rogamos confirmación* *Port Bou, 1995*

CAPITULO 7

Realia 7-1: Telephone message

1. **Reading:** Ask students to identify this piece of realia and to try to infer the meanings of phrases like **dijeron que le llamara Ud. al regresar** and **llamaría más tarde.**

2. **Reading:** Ask students to guess the meanings of several words such as **mientras, compañía,** and **recibido por.** Ask them if they can recognize the verb **estaba** as a form of **estar.**

3. **Listening/Writing:** Have students take messages. For example: **favor de llamar al señor Rodríguez lo más antes posible,** or **Julio quiere saber si te gustaría ir al museo este sábado.**

4. **Pair work/Speaking:** Have students create and then act out a business telephone call. For example: one student is a receptionist or secretary and the other is a client trying to reach an executive. The executive will be out and the receptionist will take a message.

Realia 7-2: Invitations

1. **Listening:** Before distributing copies to students, read each of the announcements aloud to see if they can guess what the celebration is.

2. **Writing:** Have students write an invitation to a ceremony or celebration of their own. It can be a religious ceremony, a birthday party, or a holiday celebration.

3. **Pair work:** Have pairs of students think of a special occasion and use the blank invitation to invite friends and/or family to a celebration. Have them present their invitations to the class.

4. **Speaking:** Have students role-play a situation in which one person invites the other to a birthday or wedding and the other either accepts or declines the invitation.

Nombre ______________________ Clase ______________ Fecha ______________

Situation Cards 7-1, 7-2, 7-3: Interview

Situation 7-1 : Interview

I call you on the telephone to talk to your brother, but he's not home. How do you answer my questions?

Aló. ¿Está tu hermano en casa?
¿Dónde está?
¿A qué hora regresa?
¿Puedo dejar un recado?

Situation 7-2: Interview

I have called to see if you are planning to come to my party. How do you respond to my questions?

¿Piensas venir a mi fiesta esta noche?
¿A qué hora vienes, a las ocho o a las nueve?
¿Estás listo/a?
¿Qué necesitas hacer antes de la fiesta?

Situation 7-3: Interview

I invite you to do several activities but you have other plans. Turn down my invitations in as many different ways as you can and explain why.

¿Te gustaría ir al parque conmigo hoy?
¿Quieres venir a mi casa esta noche?
Tengo ganas de nadar. ¿Quieres ir a la piscina ahora?
¿Prefieres ir a la piscina mañana?
Pues, ¿te gustaría ir a nadar el domingo?

Nombre ______________________ Clase ____________ Fecha ____________

Situation Cards 7-1, 7-2, 7-3: Role-playing

Situation 7-1: Role-playing

Student A When you call your best friend, **Student B** answers. Say hello and ask for your friend. Respond appropriately to the information you get from **Student B**. If your friend isn't home, tell **Student B** you will call back later and say goodbye.

Student B **Student A** calls asking for a friend. Answer the phone and tell **Student A** that you are sorry his or her friend is not home. Find out who is calling. Answer any questions **Student A** asks and respond when **Student A** says goodbye.

Situation 7-2: Role-playing

Student A You and **Student B** are about to leave for the movies. You don't want to be late but **Student B** seems to be having trouble getting ready. Ask if **Student B** is ready now and then ask what he or she needs to do. Repeat the questions until **Student B** is ready.

Student B **Student A** has arrived at your house and is anxious to leave for the movies. You are trying to stall because you and your friends have planned a surprise party for **Student A**. When **Student A** asks, keep telling him or her you aren't ready. After the third time, say you're ready.

Situation 7-3: Role-playing

Student A **Student B** is famous for making excuses not to do things. Call him or her up and extend invitations to several events or activities on the weekend. **Student B** will decline and give an excuse for not doing the activity with you.

Student B Your friend **Student A** really wants you to do something with him or her this weekend, but you have no desire or intention to do anything. You just want to stay at home and relax. Decline all invitations that **Student A** gives you and give reasons for declining.

Nombre ______________________ Clase ____________ Fecha ____________

Student Response Forms

6 Escuchemos: Por teléfono p. 183

Listen to the following telephone calls. Decide if the caller is greeting someone, saying goodbye, or unable to reach the person.

	Greeting	Goodbye	Unable to reach
1.			
2.			
3.			
4.			
5.			

9 Escuchemos: Planes p. 184

Listen to the following questions. Do these sentences answer the questions you hear? If the sentence fits as a response, check **sí**. If it doesn't, check **no**.

	Sí	No
1.		
2.		
3.		
4.		
5.		
6.		
7.		

CAPÍTULO 7

12 Escuchemos: Un sábado p. 186

It's Saturday morning and Mónica and Carlos are trying to figure out where to spend the day. Based on their conversation, where do they decide to go?

Mónica and Carlos decide to go ______________________________

19 Escuchemos: ¿Todos listos? p. 190

Listen to some members of the Garza family as they talk about getting ready at different times of the day. Based on what you hear, write the letter of the item each person would need to use in order to get ready.

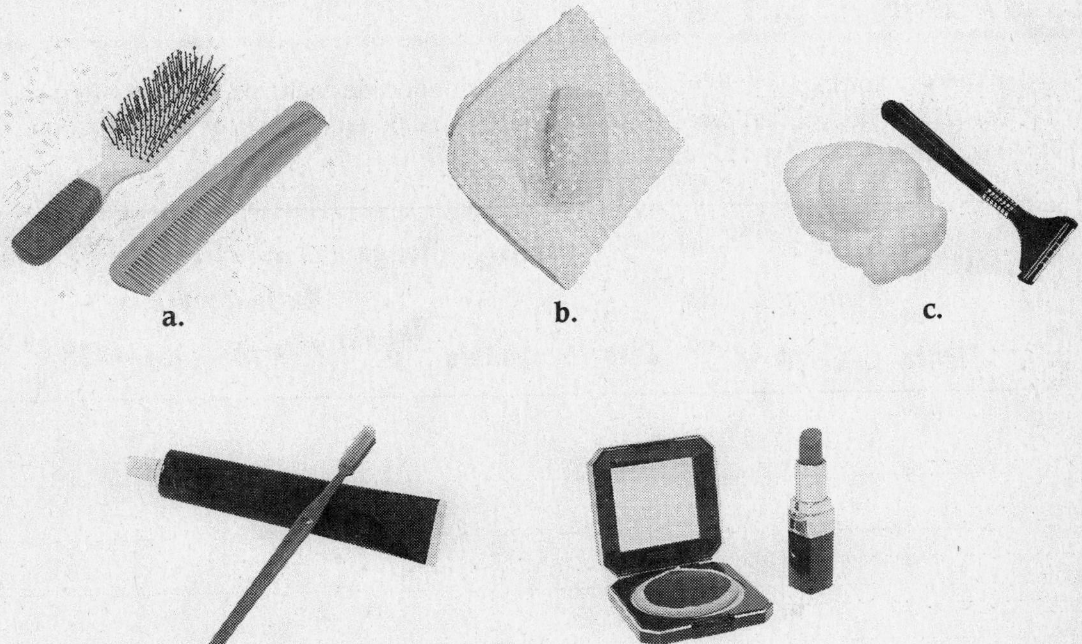

a. b. c. d. e.

1. ______
2. ______
3. ______
4. ______
5. ______

Nombre ______________________ Clase ____________ Fecha ____________

Student Response Forms

24 Escuchemos: ¿Te gustaría...? p. 193

Listen as Margarita invites several friends to go with her to do some things. Match the name of the person with his or her excuse for not being able to go.

_____ 1. Miguel
_____ 2. Mariana
_____ 3. Roberto
_____ 4. Gabriela

a. ¿Esta noche? Ay, tengo una cita esta noche.
b. ¡Qué lástima! Ya tengo planes para este fin de semana.
c. Lo siento, pero tengo que estudiar.
d. Estoy un poco cansada. Tal vez otro día, ¿eh?

Repaso Activity 3 p. 198

Listen to the following invitations and either accept or decline each one. Using the items in the word box, write your answers and be sure to use a different excuse for each situation. Try to combine some of the phrases in your answer.

Gracias, pero no puedo	Estoy cansado/a	Tengo que estudiar	Estoy enfermo/a
Tengo una cita	Tengo prisa	Ya tengo planes	
Lo siento	Tengo sueño	Estoy ocupado/a	Tal vez otro día
No tengo ganas			

1. ______________________
2. ______________________
3. ______________________
4. ______________________
5. ______________________
6. ______________________

CAPÍTULO 7

Nombre ______________________ Clase ____________ Fecha ____________

¿Qué te gustaría hacer?

Quiz 7-1

PRIMER PASO

Maximum Score: 30

I. Listening

A. Listen to Juan ask questions or make statements and choose the response that makes the most sense. (10 points)

_____ 1. **a.** Sí, pero quiero ir a la piscina también.
b. Sí, me gustaría ir al partido de fútbol.

_____ 2. **a.** Sí, vamos a la biblioteca a la una.
b. Sí, quiero estudiar con Alicia.

_____ 3. **a.** Sí, estás en la tienda.
b. Lo siento, pero está en el centro comercial.

_____ 4. **a.** No, no me gusta ir al museo.
b. Sí, me gustan los animales.

_____ 5. **a.** Claro que sí.
b. Bueno, llamo más tarde.

SCORE ______

II. Reading

B. Read this telephone conversation between Alfredo and Silvia. Then answer the questions that follow in English. (10 points)

ALFREDO Aló.
SILVIA Buenas tardes. ¿Quién habla?
ALFREDO Habla Alfredo. Hola, Silvia. ¿Quieres venir a mi casa a mirar la televisión y, después, estudiar?
SILVIA No, gracias. Pilar y yo vamos al parque de atracciones. ¿Quieres ir con nosotras?
ALFREDO Gracias, pero es imposible. Hay un examen de álgebra mañana y necesito estudiar.
SILVIA Pues, yo no tengo exámenes mañana y no necesito estudiar. El sábado voy al teatro. ¿Quieres ir conmigo?
ALFREDO Sí, ¿a qué hora empieza la obra *(play)*?
SILVIA A las dos. ¿Está bien?
ALFREDO Sí, hasta el sábado. Adiós, Silvia.

6. What does Alfredo invite Silvia to do?

____

7. Does she accept his invitation?

____

Nombre ______________________ Clase ____________ Fecha ____________

Quiz 7-1

8. What are Silvia's plans?

____

9. Why doesn't Alfredo go with Silvia and Pilar?

____

10. What plans are made for Saturday?

____

SCORE

III. Writing

C. Read the following telephone conversation between Berta and Francisco and fill in the missing information. (10 points)

11. BERTA ____.

FRANCISCO Hola, Berta. ¿Cómo estás?

BERTA ¿Quién habla?

12. FRANCISCO ____.

13. ¿____?

BERTA Lo siento, pero Luisa no está.

14. ¿____?

FRANCISCO Sí, pregúntale *(ask her)* si le gustaría ir al parque de atracciones este fin de semana. ¿A ti te gustaría ir también? Te invito.

15. BERTA ____.

FRANCISCO ¡Qué bueno! Pues, no olvides *(don't forget)* darle el recado a Silvia. Hasta luego, Berta.

BERTA Adiós.

SCORE

TOTAL SCORE /30

CAPÍTULO 7

CAPÍTULO 7

Nombre ____________________ Clase ____________ Fecha ____________

¿Qué te gustaría hacer?

Quiz 7-2

SEGUNDO PASO

Maximum Score: 35

I. Listening

A. Look at the following pictures. Listen as Arturo tells you something about each of them. Then write the letter of the picture that he describes. (10 points)

a.

b.

c.

d.

e.

1. ______ 2. ______ 3. ______ 4. ______ 5. ______

SCORE

II. Reading

B. Read the comic strip. Then indicate who is making each of the following statements by writing **Calvin** or **Mamá** in each blank. (10 points)

engrudo *paste*

te acordaras *you would remember*
Apúrate=Date prisa

Te lo pusiste *You put it*

¡Ven para acá! *Come here!*
así *this way*

__________ 6. Necesitas lavarte el pelo y luego peinarte.

__________ 7. Me gusta peinarme el pelo con engrudo.

__________ 8. Voy a tener el pelo más guapo de la escuela.

Quiz 7-2

______ 9. Pienso peinarme el pelo así todo el tiempo.

______ 10. Vamos a lavar tu pelo ahora.

SCORE

III. Writing

C. The following is a checklist on good grooming. Answer the following questions in Spanish. (10 points)

```
When do you usually need to do the following activities —
in the morning, afternoon, or evening? Or never?
```

11. comb you hair

____

12. take a shower

____

13. shave

____

14 put on makeup

____

15. brush your teeth

____

SCORE

IV. Culture

D. Based on the information in your textbook, answer **a) cierto** or **b) falso** to the statements below. (5 points)

______ 16. In Spain and Latin America, public transportation is used more frequently than private cars.

______ 17. The cost of a car is about the same all over the world.

SCORE

TOTAL SCORE /35

CAPÍTULO 7

Nombre ____________________ Clase __________ Fecha __________

¿Qué te gustaría hacer?

Quiz 7-3

TERCER PASO

Maximum Score: 35

I. Listening

A. First read the responses below. Then you'll hear five invitations. Choose the best response for each invitation. (10 points)

a. Sí, cómo no. ¿A qué hora empieza?
b. ¡Qué lástima! Me gusta la música de Smashing Pumpkins, pero tengo que trabajar.
c. Necesito estudiar más, pero no quiero. Tengo mucho sueño.
d. Lo siento, pero ya tengo planes para el sábado.
e. Me gustaría cenar contigo, pero estoy muy ocupado en casa ahora.

1. ______ 2. ______ 3. ______ 4. ______ 5. ______

SCORE

II. Reading

B. Mónica just received an invitation from Severiano for this weekend. Read her note and then answer the questions that follow in English. (10 points)

Querido Severiano,
Muchas gracias por invitarme al baile este sábado por la noche. ¡Cuánto me gustaría ir! Lo siento, pero este sábado no puedo. Tengo muchas cosas que hacer por la tarde. Mi mamá está enferma, así que tengo que cuidar a mi hermanito. También necesito estudiar para un examen y ayudar en casa. Debo pasar la aspiradora y organizar mi cuarto. Después de hacer todo eso, voy a estar cansada y no voy a tener ganas de salir. Gracias por la invitación. Tal vez otro día, ¿eh?

Tu amiga,

Mónica

6. Where does Severiano invite Monica to go and on what day?

____

____

Nombre ______________________ Clase ____________ Fecha ____________

Quiz 7-3

7. What's the main reason Monica gives for not being able to go?

____

____

8. Name two things that Monica has to do on Saturday.

____

____

9. Is Monica going to be busy during the dance itself? Explain.

____

____

10. What does Monica suggest at the end of her letter?

____

____

SCORE [ ]

III. Writing

C. You have received a lot of invitations this week! Reply to each, following the suggestion given after each one. Write your replies in Spanish. (15 points)

11. You and Catalina are invited to a dance. Accept and ask when it is.

____

12. You are invited to a baseball game. Decline because you are tired.

____

13. You are invited to go to a play. Decline because you don't feel like going to the theater.

____

14. You are invited to go swimming. Decline because you have to study.

____

15. You are invited to a birthday party. Decline because you have other plans.

____

SCORE [ ]

TOTAL SCORE [/35]

CUMULATIVE SCORE FOR QUIZZES 1–3 [/100]

CAPÍTULO 7

Nombre ______________________ Clase ____________ Fecha ____________

¿Qué te gustaría hacer?

Chapter 7 Test

I. Listening

Maximum Score: 24 points

A. Janet is having trouble with her Spanish. Listen to the sentences and help her determine the correct completion. Write the letter of the best answer. (14 points)

	a.	b.	c.
_____ 1.	a. maquillarse	b. ducharse	c. tener prisa
_____ 2.	a. enfermos	b. ocupados	c. en la boda
_____ 3.	a. tener sueño	b. tener años	c. darse prisa
_____ 4.	a. dejar un recado	b. tener ganas	c. maquillarse
_____ 5.	a. Un momento.	b. ¡Cómo no! Ya tengo planes!	c. Tal vez otro día.
_____ 6.	a. centro	b. acuario	c. parque de atracciones
_____ 7.	a. Pienso tener sueño.	b. ¡Qué lástima!	c. Voy al lago.

SCORE

B. It's going to be a busy week for Kristi. Listen to her half of a telephone conversation and write the letter of the place or event you associate with each activity she mentions. (10 points)

a. la boda
b. el baño
c. el zoológico
d. el museo
e. el teatro

8. _____ 9. _____ 10. _____ 11. _____ 12. _____

SCORE

CAPÍTULO 7

II. Reading

Maximum Score: 30 points

C. The statements below are parts of phone conversations. Indicate the matching part of each conversation with the correct letter. (10 points)

_____ 13. ¿Puedo hablar con Ricardo, por favor?
_____ 14. Su línea personal está ocupada, señora.
_____ 15. Bueno, Marta. ¿Quieres ir al circo mañana?
_____ 16. ¿Puedo hablar con la Sra. Salinas?
_____ 17. ¿Te gustaría ir al lago?

a. Claro que sí. ¿A qué hora?
b. Un momento. Lo siento, pero la línea está ocupada.
c. Él no está. ¿Quieres dejar un recado?
d. ¿Puedo dejar un recado?
e. ¡Cómo no! Me gustan mucho los deportes de agua.

SCORE

Chapter 7 Test

D. Read the phone conversation below and choose the best answer to the questions that follow. (10 points)

ALONSO Aló. ¿Está Pedro?
JUAN Lo siento, pero no está. ¿Puedes llamar más tarde?
ALONSO Sí, pero no tengo mucho tiempo. ¿Les gustaría a Uds. venir a mi casa en media hora?
JUAN ¿Por qué?
ALONSO Hay una fiesta de cumpleaños a las nueve. Es una fiesta de sorpresa para María.
JUAN Pues, no puedo. Ya tengo planes, pero tal vez Pedro pueda ir.
ALONSO Favor de decirle a Pedro que hay una fiesta.

Pedro returns Alonso's call.

PEDRO Aló. ¿Alonso?
ALONSO Sí, soy yo. ¿Qué hay de nuevo?
PEDRO Juan dice que hay una fiesta esta noche.
ALONSO Sí, para María. ¿Quieres venir?
PEDRO ¡Cómo no! ¿A qué hora empieza la fiesta?
ALONSO A las nueve.
PEDRO Pues, primero tengo que afeitarme.
ALONSO Está bien. Chao, hasta las nueve.

_____ **18.** Alonso is telling Juan about . . .
- **a.** a party for María
- **b.** his plans for the weekend

_____ **19.** . . . will not be seeing Alonso this evening
- **a.** Pedro
- **b.** Juan

_____ **20.** Pedro needs to . . .
- **a.** call Alonso back
- **b.** shave

_____ **21.** Juan and Pedro . . .
- **a.** are either brothers or close friends
- **b.** have not met yet

_____ **22.** . . . is going to get a big surprise soon.
- **a.** María
- **b.** Pedro

SCORE ______

CAPÍTULO 7

E. It's Friday evening and Tulio is telling his aunt Sofía about his plans for tonight. Read their conversation, then mark the statements that follow **a) cierto** or **b) falso**. (10 points)

TÍA SOFÍA ¿Qué piensas hacer esta noche, hijo?
TULIO Meche y yo pensamos cenar primero en el Taco Loco y después vamos a ver una película.
TÍA SOFÍA ¿Y a qué hora debes estar en su casa?
TULIO No voy a su casa. Ella viene aquí con sus padres a las siete y cuarto porque ellos pasan por aquí cuando van a la reunión de la familia Perea.
TÍA SOFÍA ¿A las siete y cuarto? Pero hijo, ya son las siete. ¿Estás listo?
TULIO No, todavía necesito peinarme.
TÍA SOFÍA ¿No vas a ducharte primero?
TULIO Bueno, sí, tía. Creo que debo ducharme.
TÍA SOFÍA Entonces, ¡date prisa, hombre! Ya es tarde.
TULIO Ah, y tía Sofía, ¿me puede planchar la ropa rápidamente, por favor?
TÍA SOFÍA ¡Plancharte la ropa! ¿En quince minutos? No, hijo, lo siento, pero no puedo... ¡Yo también tengo mis planes para esta noche!

_____ 23. Tulio y Meche van al cine esta noche.

_____ 24. Tulio tiene que estar listo en una hora.

_____ 25. Tía Sofía no tiene nada que hacer esta noche.

_____ 26. Tulio necesita ducharse y peinarse.

_____ 27. Tía Sofía va a planchar la ropa de Tulio.

SCORE

CAPÍTULO 7

III. Culture

Maximum Score: 4 points

F. Read the statements below. Based on the information in your textbook, determine whether the statements are **a) cierto** or **b) falso**. (4 points)

_____ 28. Having a driver's license at age 16 is common in Latin American countries, as it is in the United States.

_____ 29. Boys in many Spanish-speaking countries typically pay when going out on dates with girls.

SCORE

Nombre ________________________ Clase ____________ Fecha ____________

Chapter 7 Test

IV. Writing

Maximum Score: 42 points

G. Using the cues below, write two sentences in Spanish for each picture. In the first sentence, say the person is not yet ready. In the second sentence, say what the person has to do to get ready. (15 points)

30. Ella ______________________________

31. Él ______________________________

32. Nosotras ______________________________

33. Yo ______________________________

34. Tú ______________________________

SCORE ______

CAPÍTULO 7

H. Your friend Carolina just invited you to a party tomorrow night, but you already have plans. Write a letter to Carolina thanking her for inviting you and declining the invitation. (11 points)

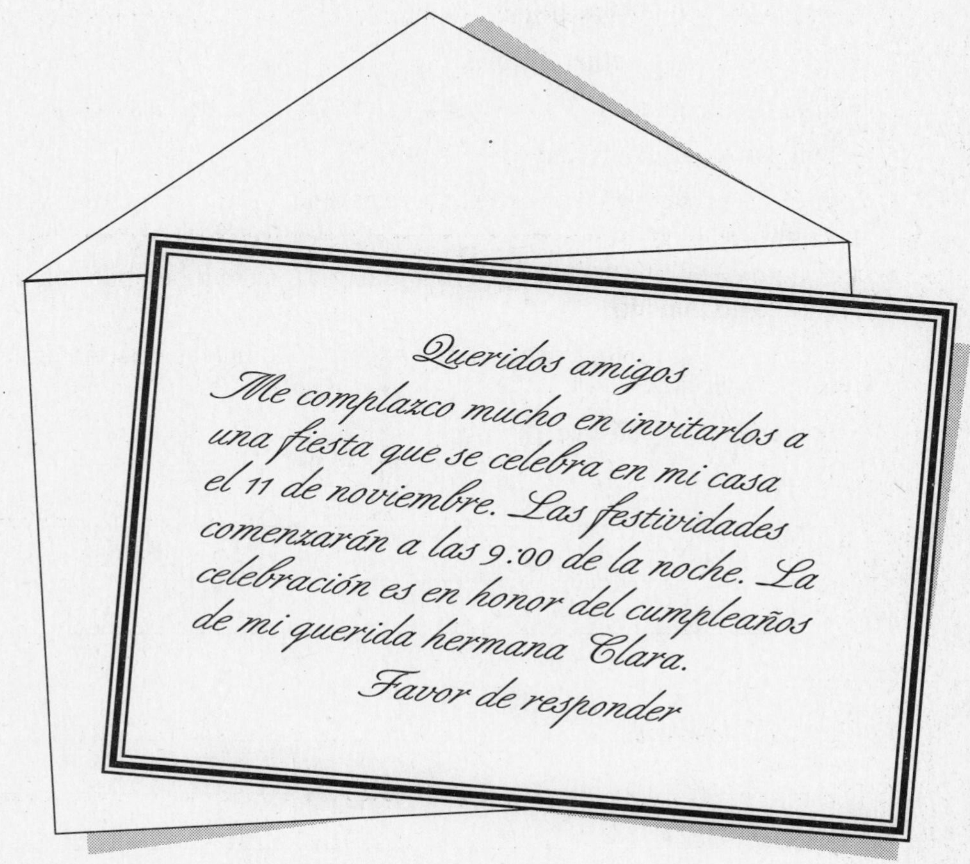

Queridos amigos

Me complazco mucho en invitarlos a una fiesta que se celebra en mi casa el 11 de noviembre. Las festividades comenzarán a las 9:00 de la noche. La celebración es en honor del cumpleaños de mi querida hermana Clara.

Favor de responder

35. ____

____

____

____

____

____

____

____

____

SCORE ____

Chapter 7 Test

I. Write an eight-line phone dialogue in which your friend calls you to invite you to the movies. Your dialogue should include the following: (16 points)

- Typical telephone greetings.
- You ask how the other is doing.
- Your friend asks you if you would like to go to the movies tonight.
- You ask what movie and what time.
- Your friend says which movie and what time. (Think of a movie you would like to see and make up a time.)
- You thank your friend but say that you can't make it because you have a lot to do tonight.
- Your friend says it's a shame and suggests that maybe you can go some other day.
- You both say good-bye.

36. TÚ ______________________________
37. AMIGO ______________________________
38. TÚ ______________________________
39. AMIGO ______________________________
40. TÚ ______________________________
41. AMIGO ______________________________
42. TÚ ______________________________
43. AMIGO ______________________________

SCORE ______

TOTAL SCORE ______ /100

Nombre ______________________ Clase ____________ Fecha ____________

CAPÍTULO 7 Chapter Test Score Sheet

Circle the letter that matches the most appropriate answer.

I. Listening

Maximum Score: 24 points

A. (14 points)

1. a b c
2. a b c
3. a b c
4. a b c
5. a b c
6. a b c
7. a b c

B. (10 points)

8. a b c d e
9. a b c d e
10. a b c d e
11. a b c d e
12. a b c d e

SCORE ☐

II. Reading

Maximum Score: 30 points

C. (10 points)

13. a b c d e
14. a b c d e
15. a b c d e
16. a b c d e
17. a b c d e

SCORE ☐

D. (10 points)

18. a b
19. a b
20. a b
21. a b
22. a b

SCORE ☐

E. (10 points)

23. a b
24. a b
25. a b
26. a b
27. a b

SCORE ☐

III. Culture

Maximum Score: 4 points

F. (4 points)

28. a b
29. a b

SCORE ☐

IV. Writing

Maximum Score: 42 points

G. (15 points)

30. ______________________

31. ______________________

32. ______________________

33. ______________________

34. ______________________

SCORE

H. (11 points)

35. ______________________

SCORE

I. (16 points)

36. TÚ ______________________
37. AMIGO ______________________
38. TÚ ______________________
39. AMIGO ______________________
40. TÚ ______________________
41. AMIGO ______________________
42. TÚ ______________________
43. AMIGO ______________________

SCORE

TOTAL SCORE /100

RESOURCES

Scripts and Answers

CAPÍTULO 7

Scripts for Additional Listening Activities

Additional Listening Activity 7-1, p. 127

1. ¿Diga?
2. Lo siento, no está.
3. ¿Quién habla?
4. ¿Quieres dejar un recado?
5. La línea está ocupada.
6. Bueno.
7. ¿De parte de quién, por favor?

Additional Listening Activity 7-2, p. 127

TÍA ISABEL Hola, todos. Habla tía Isabel. Este recado es para todos. Escuchen, quiero organizar una fiesta de sorpresa para abuela. Me gustaría hacer la fiesta este sábado. Por favor, llámenme más tarde en casa, al cuatro, cincuenta y uno, cincuenta y seis, treinta y tres. Es urgente. Hasta luego.

GONZALO Este... hola, muy buenas. Habla Gonzalo Rayas y este recado es para Sonia. Sonia, no me conoces muy bien, pero estoy en tu clase de química. Soy el chico bajo y moreno. Este... bueno, ¿te gustaría ir conmigo al baile este viernes? Te llamo más tarde. Hasta luego.

TERESA Hola, buenas tardes. Habla Teresa y este recado es para Verónica. Oye, Verónica, por favor, ¿puedes ayudarme a estudiar esta noche para el examen de inglés? Necesito tu ayuda. Por favor, llámame al cuatro, cincuenta y nueve, treinta y cuatro, cuarenta y cinco. ¡Es urgente! Gracias, chica.

Additional Listening Activity 7-3, p. 128

1. PEPE Marisa, ¿qué vas a hacer esta noche?
MARISA Voy a salir con mis primos. Vamos a un concierto.
2. PEPE Héctor, ¿qué planes tienes el sábado por la tarde?
HÉCTOR Voy a ir al lago con mi amigo Martín. Vamos a nadar.
3. PEPE Anita, ¿qué planes tienes para el domingo por la noche?
ANITA ¡Tengo que acompañar a mi hermanito al circo! ¡El circo! ¡Qué aburrido!
4. PEPE Sergio, ¿qué haces mañana por la mañana?
SERGIO Bueno, pienso ir al campo con mi hermano mayor.
5. PEPE Lupe, ¿qué vas a hacer el domingo por la tarde?
LUPE Bueno, voy a la casa de mis tíos. Hay una fiesta para celebrar su aniversario de bodas.

Additional Listening Activity 7-4, p. 128

1. ANA ¿Estás listo, Joaquín?
JOAQUÍN Todavía no. Necesito afeitarme.
ANA Joaquín, sólo tienes trece años. No eres como papá. No vas a tener que afeitarte por mucho tiempo todavía.
JOAQUÍN No es cierto. ¡Necesito afeitarme por lo menos una vez a la semana!
ANA Bueno, date prisa. La película empieza a las ocho.
2. GERALDO ¿Aurelia? Aurelia, ¿dónde estás?
AURELIA Perdón. No estoy lista todavía.
GERALDO Pero, cariño... el concierto empieza a las ocho y media y ya son las ocho y diez.
AURELIA No te preocupes. Sólo necesito maquillarme.
GERALDO Pero para maquillarte necesitas por lo menos media hora...

3. LUISA ¿Carlos? ¿Qué haces? Los invitados van a llegar dentro de poco.
CARLOS Estoy casi listo, sólo necesito peinarme.
LUISA Muy bien, pues. Tenemos mucho que hacer.

4. MAMÁ Víctor, nos vamos ahora mismo. Tu cita con el dentista es a las cinco en punto.
VÍCTOR Ya voy, mamá.
MAMÁ Oye, Víctor, tienes que lavarte bien los dientes antes, ¿eh?
VÍCTOR Sí, sí, mamá. Voy a lavármelos ahora.

Additional Listening Activity 7-5, p. 129

1. MARCOS Hola, Elisa, ¿eres tú? Soy yo, Marcos.
ELISA Marcos, ¿cómo estás?
MARCOS Bien, gracias. Sólo quería saber si vas al picnic del club.
ELISA Ah, sí, el picnic... ¿Cuándo es?
MARCOS Mañana, a la una.
ELISA Ay, Marcos, perdóname, pero no puedo ir. Mañana tengo que ir a la boda de mi prima Susana.
MARCOS ¡Ay, qué lástima!
ELISA Sí, lo sé. Que lo pasen muy bien.
MARCOS Hasta luego.

---

2. SR. SOTO ¿Diga?
MARCOS Hola. ¿Está Cristóbal, por favor?
SR. SOTO ¿Quién habla?
MARCOS Soy yo, Marcos. ¿Cómo está, Sr. Soto?
SR. SOTO Ah, Marcos. Bien, gracias. Sí, Cristóbal está. Espera un momento.
CRISTÓBAL ¿Marcos?
MARCOS Hola, Cristóbal. Oye, ¿vas al picnic mañana?
CRISTÓBAL Sí, claro. Es a la una, ¿verdad?
MARCOS Sí, en el parque.
CRISTÓBAL Bueno, nos vemos allí. Hasta mañana.

---

3. MARISOL ¿Diga?
MARCOS Hola, ¿Marisol? Habla Marcos.
MARISOL Marcos, ¿qué tal?
MARCOS Muy bien, gracias. Oye, Marisol... vas a nuestro picnic mañana, ¿verdad?
MARISOL Bueno, depende. Me gustaría ir, pero mi prima Rosaura está aquí de visita. No quiero dejarla sola en casa.
MARCOS No te preocupes. Si ella quiere, puede venir también. Tenemos mucha comida.
MARISOL Ah, perfecto. Entonces, sí vamos las dos.
MARCOS Muy bien. Hasta mañana.

---

4. CÉSAR ¿Hola?
MARCOS César, ¿eres tú? Soy Marcos.
CÉSAR Hola, hombre. ¿Qué hay?
MARCOS Nada... sólo quiero recordarte que mañana es el picnic del club.
CÉSAR ¿Es mañana? ¿No es el domingo?
MARCOS No, no. Es mañana a la una. ¿Por qué?
CÉSAR Marcos, lo siento mucho, pero no puedo ir al picnic ahora. Tengo planes para el sábado. Voy con mis padres al campo a visitar a mis abuelos.
MARCOS Qué lástima. Bueno, hasta el lunes.

Additional Listening Activity 7-6, p. 129

1. ¿Te gustaría ir conmigo al teatro mañana? Vamos a la ópera.
2. ¿Tienes ganas de venir a mi casa? Vamos a jugar a las cartas.
3. Oye, ¿quieres ir a tomar un helado ahora?
4. Oye, Fernando y yo vamos a hacer un viaje al campo mañana. ¿Te gustaría venir?
5. Esta noche vamos al cine para ver esa nueva película. ¿Quieres ir?
6. ¿Tienes ganas de ir conmigo a cenar en ese restaurante chino nuevo?

Answers to Additional Listening Activities

Additional Listening Activity 7-1, p. 127

1. a
2. b
3. b
4. a
5. b
6. a
7. a

Additional Listening Activity 7-2, p. 127

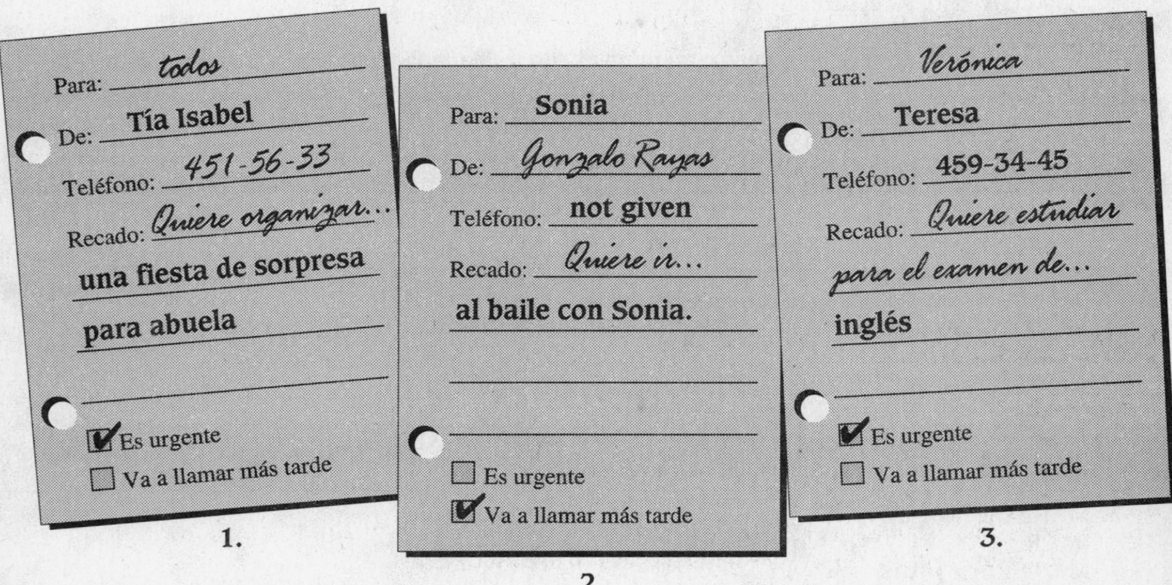

Additional Listening Activity 7-3, p. 128

1. Marisa: va al concierto con sus primos
2. Héctor: va al lago con su amigo Martín
3. Anita: va al circo con su hermanito
4. Sergio: va al campo con su hermano mayor
5. Lupe: va a la fiesta de aniversario de sus tíos

Additional Listening Activity 7-4, p. 128

1. b 2. a 3. b 4. a

Additional Listening Activity 7-5, p. 129

Elisa: no; tiene que ir a una boda
Cristóbal: sí
Marisol: sí
César: no; tiene que visitar a sus abuelos

Additional Listening Activity 7-6, p. 129

1. a 2. a 3. b 4. a 5. a 6. b

Listening Scripts for Quizzes

Quiz 7-1 Capítulo 7 Primer paso

I. Listening

A.
1. ¿Te gustaría jugar al voleibol esta tarde?
2. ¿Quieres estudiar conmigo?
3. Me gustaría hablar con Claudia. ¿Está en casa?
4. ¿Te gustaría ir al zoológico?
5. Lo siento, pero Benito no está.

Quiz 7-2 Capítulo 7 Segundo paso

I. Listening

A.
1. El señor Martínez necesita afeitarse todos los días.
2. Juanita no está lista. Todavía debe maquillarse.
3. Gloria piensa ducharse todas las noches.
4. El señor Gómez necesita lavarse los dientes.
5. Luisa va a un baile más tarde; por eso tiene que peinarse.

Quiz 7-3 Capítulo 7 Tercer paso

I. Listening

A.
1. ¿Tienes ganas de cenar en mi casa esta noche?
2. ¿Te gustaría ir al partido de béisbol mañana?
3. ¿Quieres ir a tomar un refresco el sábado?
4. ¿Tienes que estudiar esta noche?
5. María quiere ir al concierto. ¿Quieres ir con nosotros?

Answers to Quizzes 7-1, 7-2, 7-3

ANSWERS Quiz 7-1

I. Listening

A. (10 points: 2 points per item)
1. a
2. a
3. b
4. b
5. b

II. Reading

B. (10 points: 2 points per item)
6. Alfredo invites Silvia to come to his house to watch TV and study.
7. No.
8. Silvia is going to the amusement park with Pilar.
9. Alfredo needs to study for an algebra test.
10. Silvia and Alfredo plan to go to the theater.

III. Writing

C. (10 points: 2 points per item)
Answers will vary. Possible answers:
11. Diga
12. Soy yo, Francisco
13. Puedo hablar con Luisa
14. Quieres dejarle un recado
15. Claro que sí

ANSWERS Quiz 7-2

I. Listening

A. (10 points: 2 points per item)
1. b
2. d
3. e
4. a
5. c

II. Reading

B. (10 points: 2 points per item)
6. Mamá
7. Calvin
8. Calvin
9. Calvin
10. Mamá

III. Writing

C. (10 points: 2 points per item)
Answers will vary. Possible answers:
11. Necesito peinarme por la mañana antes de ir al colegio.
12. Necesito ducharme por la noche después de jugar al béisbol.
13. Necesito afeitarme por la mañana.
14. Necesito maquillarme por la noche antes de ir a una fiesta.
15. Necesito lavarme los dientes por la mañana, por la tarde y por la noche.

IV. Culture

D. (5 points: 2 $1/2$ points per item)
16. a 17. b

ANSWERS Quiz 7-3

I. Listening

A. (10 points: 2 points per item)
1. e
2. a
3. d
4. c
5. b

II. Reading

B. (10 points: 2 points per item)
Answers will vary. Possible answers:
6. Severiano invites Monica to a dance on Saturday night.
7. Monica has a lot to do on Saturday.
8. Monica has to vacuum and clean her room.
9. No, but Monica's probably going to be tired and not interested in going out.
10. She suggests that maybe they can go out some other day.

III. Writing

C. (15 points: 3 points per item)
Answers will vary. Possible answers:
11. Sí, cómo no. ¿Cuándo es?
12. Gracias, pero no puedo porque estoy cansado/a.
13. Lo siento, pero no tengo ganas de ir al teatro esta noche.
14. No puedo porque tengo que estudiar.
15. Gracias, pero no puedo. Ya tengo planes.

Scripts for Chapter Test Capítulo 7

I. Listening

A. 1. Después de jugar al béisbol, Luis debe ________.
2. Ellos no pueden ir porque no están bien. Creo que están ________.
3. Mi mamá no tiene mucho tiempo. Pienso que debe ________.
4. —¡Aló! ¿Está Marcela?
—No, no está. ¿Quieres ________?
5. ¿Tienes ganas de ir al concierto conmigo?
6. Nos gustan mucho los animales que viven en el agua. Vamos al ________.
7. ¿Qué piensas hacer esta tarde?

B ¡Hola, María! Sí, soy yo... ¿Cómo estás?... Yo bien, gracias.[...] No, no puedo ir contigo a ver los nuevos elefantes blancos. [...] Lo siento pero el viernes tampoco puedo. Voy con mis padres a ver la exposición de arte antigua. [...] ¿El sábado? También estoy ocupada. [...] Sí, se casa mi hermana Julia. María, espera un momento. Mi hermano Manuel se está duchando y necesita una toalla... Hola. Ya estoy aquí. [...] Sí. Creo que el martes es un buen día para ir a ver esa nueva comedia musical. ¡Qué buena idea!

Answers to Chapter Test

I. Listening Maximum Score: 24 points

A. (14 points: 2 points per item)
1. b
2. a
3. c
4. a
5. c
6. b
7. c

B. (10 points: 2 points per item)
8. c
9. d
10. a
11. b
12. e

II. Reading Maximum Score: 30 points

C. (10 points: 2 points per item)
13. c
14. d
15. a
16. b
17. e

D. (10 points: 2 points per item)
18. a
19. b
20. b
21. a
22. a

E. (10 points: 2 points per item)
23. a
24. b
25. b
26. a
27. b

III. Culture Maximum Score: 4 points

F. (4 points: 2 points per item)
28. b **29.** a

IV. Writing Maximum Score: 42 points

G. (15 points: 3 points per item)
Answers will vary. Possible answers:
30. Ella no está lista. Tiene que lavarse los dientes.
31. Él no está listo. Tiene que afeitarse.
32. Nosotras no estamos listas. Tenemos que maquillarnos.
33. Yo no estoy listo. Tengo que ducharme.
34. Tú no estás listo. Tienes que peinarte.

H. (11 points)
Answers will vary. Possible answer:
35. Querida Carolina, Muchas gracias por la invitación. Lo siento mucho, pero no puedo venir a la fiesta. Es que ya tengo planes. Voy a salir con mis amigos.

I. (16 points: 2 points per item)
Dialogues will vary. Possible dialogue:
36. ¿Diga?
37. Hola Pablo, ¿cómo estás?
38. Muy bien, ¿y tú?
39. Bien. Oye, ¿quieres ir al cine conmigo?
40. ¿Qué película y a qué hora?
41. Quiero ver (*película*) a las (*hora*).
42. Lo siento, pero no puedo. Tal vez otro día.
43. ¡Qué lástima! Bueno, hasta luego.

¿Qué te gustaría hacer?

DE ANTEMANO

1 Write the name of the **fotonovela** character next to each statement that he or she could have made. Choose from the following characters: Diego, Cristina, Pablo, or Sr. Andrade.

Diego 1. ¿Por qué Cristina no me invita a su fiesta? Somos buenos amigos...

Pablo 2. ¡Pobre Diego! Está muy triste. Me gustaría ayudar...

Cristina 3. ¡Qué pena! Pablo no puede ir a mi fiesta.

Sr. Andrade 4. ¿Dónde debo poner este recado para Diego? Ah... aquí en la mesa está bien.

Pablo 5. ¡Qué complicado! Me gustaría ir a la fiesta de Cristina, pero ya tengo planes con Diego.

2 Greg, a new exchange student in Ecuador, has a really busy week planned. Based on his calendar below, match each invitation with the correct response.

lunes	martes	miércoles	jueves	viernes	sábado	domingo
4	5	6	7	8	9	10
Reunión—Club de intercambio, 6:00 p.m.	*Cita—Dr. Londoño, 4:30 p.m.*	*Concierto, 9:30 p.m.*	*Cita—Oficina del Director, 10:00 a.m.*	*Examen de español, 9:00 a.m.*	*Fiesta—Cristina Ordóñez, 8:30 p.m.*	*Fútbol—parque, 12:30 p.m.*

e 1. ¿Quieres ir al cine esta noche a las seis?

a 2. ¿Cuándo es tu examen de español?

d 3. Vamos al zoológico este domingo. ¿Quieres ir también?

b 4. ¿Te gustaría venir a mi casa mañana después de clases?

f 5. Oye, vamos a ir a tomar algo ahora durante el descanso. ¿Quieres ir?

c 6. ¿Qué planes tienes para el sábado?

a. Es el viernes a las nueve. ¡Necesito estudiar y practicar mucho esta semana!

b. Lo siento, pero no puedo. Mañana tengo una cita con el médico a las cuatro y media de la tarde.

c. Por la noche voy a la fiesta de Cristina.

d. Creo que el domingo voy a jugar al fútbol. Pero gracias, ¿eh?

e. Gracias, pero a las seis voy a una reunión del Club de intercambio.

f. ¿Van ahora mismo? Lo siento, pero tengo que hablar con el director a las diez.

Practice and Activity Book p. 73

PRIMER PASO

3 Below are parts of two phone conversations. Use the new words and expressions on p. 183 of your textbook to complete the missing parts of the conversations.

Answers will vary. Possible answers:

Manuel

MANUEL ¿Aló?

ELENA 1. **Buenas tardes. ¿Está Leonor, por favor?**

MANUEL ¿De parte de quién, por favor?

ELENA 2. **Soy yo, Elena.**

MANUEL Elena ¿qué tal? Oye, lo siento, pero no está ahora.

ELENA 3. **¿Puedo dejar un recado?**

MANUEL Está bien.

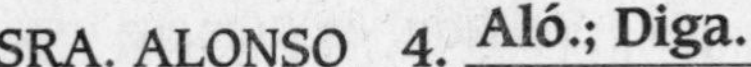

SRA. ALONSO 4. **Aló.; Diga.**

LEONOR Buenos días, Sra. Alonso. ¿Está Carmen, por favor?

SRA. ALONSO 5. **¿Quién habla?**

LEONOR Soy yo, Leonor.

SRA. ALONSO 6. **¿Cómo estás, Leonor?**

LEONOR Muy bien, gracias. ¿Y Ud.?

SRA. ALONSO 7. **Muy bien, gracias. Oye, Carmen no está ahora.**

LEONOR No hay problema. Llamo más tarde.

SRA. ALONSO 8. **Ella regresa a las cinco.**

LEONOR Bien. **Adiós**, Sra. Alonso.

SRA. ALONSO Adiós.

Leonor

4 Sometimes Calvin answers the phone at his house and the results are not always what the callers expect. Read the following comic strip, then answer the questions.

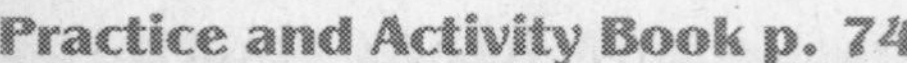

Practice and Activity Book p. 74

1. What does the caller want? **He wants to talk to Calvin's dad.**

2. Does Calvin help the caller? **No, not really.**

3. Who do you think is calling in the last frame?
It's the same person, calling back.

4. Imagine that the speech bubble in the third frame of the comic strip is empty. What could Calvin say in response to the caller's question that would be more helpful?
Answers will vary. Possible answers: ¿De parte de quién, por favor?; ¿Quién habla, por favor?; Un momento, por favor.; ¿Quiere Ud. dejar un recado?

5 What would you invite the people shown below to do? Create an invitation for each one, based on what you think each person or group of people likes to do. Then write the other person's acceptance of the invitation. **Answers will vary. Possible answers:**

1. TÚ **¿Te gustaría ir al lago conmigo este fin de semana?**
   TU AMIGO **¡Claro que sí! Me gusta pescar.**

2. TÚ **¿Les gustaría correr conmigo en el parque?**
   TUS AMIGOS **Sí, nos gusta correr.**

3. TÚ **¿Les gustaría jugar al tenis esta tarde?**
   TUS AMIGAS **¡Claro! Nos gustaría jugar contigo.**

4. TÚ **¿Te gustaría ir a un concierto mañana?**
   TU AMIGO **Sí, me gusta escuchar música.**

5. TÚ **¿Quieren ver la televisión esta noche conmigo?**
   TUS AMIGOS **Sí, hay una película muy buena.**

6 Use the clues and the **Vocabulario** section on p. 186 of your textbook to complete the following sentences.

1. El lugar donde puedes ver animales acuáticos es el **acuario**.
2. Un lugar donde viven muchas personas, por ejemplo Quito o Miami, es una **ciudad**.
3. Cuando una persona termina las clases en el colegio, a veces hay una **fiesta de graduación** para celebrar.
4. Un lugar muy divertido, donde hay montañas rusas *(rollercoasters)*, es el **parque de atracciones**.
5. La ceremonia en que un hombre y una mujer se casan *(marry)* es una **boda**.
6. Una fiesta para celebrar 50 años de matrimonio *(marriage)* es una **fiesta de aniversario**.
7. El lugar lejos de las ciudades donde es posible ver la naturaleza *(nature)*, es el **campo**.
8. Ahora tengo 14 años. En junio, voy a cumplir 15 y voy a tener una **fiesta de cumpleaños**.
9. El lugar donde puedes ver actores en una comedia es el **teatro**.
10. Mis padres se casaron en 1985 y ahora van a tener una fiesta de **aniversario**.

7 Where would the people below rather go this weekend, and why? Write a sentence about each person's preferences based on the drawings.

MODELO

Mario prefiere ir al circo porque quiere ver los elefantes.

Answers will vary. Possible answers:

1. Esteban y Ramón
Esteban y Ramón prefieren ir al parque de atracciones porque es muy divertido.

2. El Sr. Arco

El Sr. Arco prefiere ir al museo de antropología porque le gusta la historia.

3. La familia Tamayo
La familia Tamayo prefiere ir al zoológico porque a su hija le gustan los animales.

4. Nosotros
Nosotros preferimos ir al lago porque queremos nadar.

SEGUNDO PASO

8 Some classmates are talking about weekend plans in the cafeteria. Read what each person has planned, then draw a line connecting the pairs of students that are going to do something together.

1. Más que nada, quiero ver los leones y los tigres, pero los elefantes son muy interesantes también.
2. Voy a pasar el sábado con mi amigo Felipe. Vamos al lago, ¡y nos vamos a divertir muchísimo!
3. Mi grupo favorito "Sabor tropical" va a tocar este sábado. ¡Son increíbles!
4. Antonio tiene dos entradas *(tickets)* para el nuevo parque de atracciones. Me encantan los parques de atracciones. ¡Pienso subir a la montaña rusa *(rollercoaster)* 50 veces!

a. Hay tantas cosas que hacer allí. Pienso nadar y tomar el sol.

b. Me gustaría mucho salir con Marisol este fin de semana. Ella quiere ir al parque de atracciones, pero a mí la montaña rusa no me gusta.

c. Mi prima Juanita y yo pensamos ir al zoológico el domingo. A ella le fascinan los animales.

d. Creo que Amalia y yo vamos a salir. Pensamos asistir a un concierto de música caribeña en el Teatro Central.

9 Araceli and Manolo are planning what they're going to do this weekend. Complete their conversation with the correct forms of the following verbs.

gustaría pensar querer ir preferir

MANOLO Oye, Araceli, ¿qué **piensas** hacer este fin de semana?

ARACELI Pues, no sé. ¿Qué **vas** a hacer tú?

MANOLO Bueno, (yo) **quiero** ir al lago, pero mis hermanitos **quieren** jugar al tenis conmigo. Pero no me gusta mucho jugar al tenis; **prefiero/quiero** nadar. ¿Te **gustaría** ir al lago conmigo?

ARACELI Sí, me **gustaría**... pero, ¿cuándo **piensas** ir? **Prefiero** ir el sábado porque el domingo por la tarde **voy** al museo con Guillermo.

10 Emilio is talking to Alejandra about weekend plans. Using the expressions **ir** + **a** + infinitive and **pensar** + infinitive, write what Emilio would say about his plans, how he would ask about Alejandra's plans, and what she would say Víctor and the other two boys are planning to do.

MODELO

Amador

Amador va a ir al parque este fin de semana. Piensa jugar al fútbol con sus amigos.

Answers will vary. Possible answers:

1. Emilio

Voy a ir a un restaurante mexicano este fin de semana. Pienso cenar con mi amiga Teresa.

2. Alejandra

¿Y tú, Alejandra? ¿ **Tienes planes para este fin de semana** ?

¿ **Piensas ir al lago para nadar** ?

3. Víctor

Víctor no va a salir de casa este fin de semana. Piensa descansar y dormir.

4. Rafa y José Luis

Rafa y José Luis van a ir al parque de atracciones este fin de semana. Piensan hacer muchas cosas divertidas.

Practice and Activity Book p. 78

11 This Saturday Gustavo has a lot of plans. Write at least five sentences describing his day, using the illustrations as a guide and the expressions in the box below.

- ir + a + ...
- pensar + ...
- necesitar + ...
- querer + ...
- A Gustavo le gustaría + ...

Answers will vary.

12 The Montemayors are going out with some friends tonight. Complete the following sentences with what each person needs to do to get ready according to the cues. Start with Mrs. Montemayor asking her husband if everyone is ready.

1. ¿ **Están listos todos** ?
2. No, mi amor. Marco **necesita lavarse los dientes.**
3. Y yo **necesito afeitarme.**
4. Creo que tú **necesitas maquillarte.**
5.  Luego Marisa **necesita peinarse.**
6.  Y por último, Pepe **necesita ducharse.**

TERCER PASO

13 The strip below shows a conversation between Calvin and his friend Susi. Read the cartoon, then answer the questions.

1. Hobbes is Calvin's toy tiger. Where is Hobbes in the strip above?
   Hobbes is having tea with Susi and her toy rabbit.
2. What phrase does Susi use in the second scene to extend an invitation to Calvin ?
   ¿No quieres venir a tomar el té?
3. What's his answer and why do you think he answers this way?
   He says no because he's busy looking for Hobbes.
4. What does Susi think of Calvin because of the way he answered?
   She thinks he's rude.

14 How else could Calvin have responded to Susi's invitation? Imagine that you are the cartoonist, and create three new responses for Calvin.

a. an acceptance **Answers will vary.**

b. a refusal with an excuse

c. a suggestion that he and Susi do something else

15 Luisa and Marcos were passing notes to each other in study hall. Match up what Marcos wrote on the left with Luisa's sentences on the right. Number Luisa's sentences in the correct order to find out what they were discussing. When you finish, read through the note in order and answer the questions below.

	Marcos		Luisa
1.	¿Qué vas a hacer este sábado?	4	Bueno, ¿te gustaría estudiar conmigo? A mí me gusta el álgebra.
3.	Porque tengo que hacer la tarea de álgebra y es muy difícil.	8	Buena idea... siempre tengo ganas de comer algo después de estudiar.
5.	¿En serio? Gracias... me gustaría mucho. ¿A qué hora quieres estudiar?	2	Por la mañana, nada, pero por la tarde, voy a salir. ¿Por qué?
7.	¡Perfecto! Y después, si quieres, vamos a comer una hamburguesa.	6	No sé... ¿Por qué no vienes a mi casa a las diez? Así podemos estudiar juntos.

16 Based of the information in Activity 15 indicate whether each statement is true or false. Correct the false ones.

1. Luisa no tiene planes para el sábado.
   Falso. Luisa tiene planes para el sábado por la tarde.
2. Marcos tiene que estudiar para un examen de historia.
   Falso. Él tiene que hacer la tarea de álgebra.
3. Marcos y Luisa piensan estudiar juntos el sábado por la mañana.
   Cierto.
4. Después de estudiar con Luisa, Marcos tiene prisa para ir al trabajo.
   Falso. Ellos van a comer algo después de estudiar.
5. Luisa siempre tiene sueño después de estudiar.
   Falso. Ella siempre tiene ganas de comer algo después de estudiar.

17 Joaquín has just called some friends to come over and watch videos this afternoon. Based on what you see in the pictures, how do his friends respond? Include Joaquín's invitation and his friends' excuses in each conversation. Use the following expressions: **tener que** + infinitive, **tener sueño**, **(no) tener ganas de** + infinitive, and **tener prisa**.

Jimena

Juanito

Fernanda

Roberto

JOAQUÍN **Answers will vary. Possible answers:**

Hola, Jimena. Soy yo, Joaquín. ¿Te gustaría venir a mi casa y ver unos videos?

JIMENA **Ay, Joaquín. Muchas gracias, pero no puedo. Estoy muy cansada y tengo sueño. Tal vez otro día.**

JOAQUÍN **Hola, Juanito. Habla Joaquín. Oye, ¿tienes ganas de venir a mi casa y ver unos videos?**

JUANITO **Me gustaría mucho, hombre, pero es imposible. Tengo que hacer muchas cosas en casa.**

JOAQUÍN **Hola, Fernanda. Soy Joaquín. ¿Quieres venir a mi casa esta tarde y ver unos videos?**

FERNANDA **Ay, Joaquín. Lo siento mucho, pero tengo mucha prisa. Vamos a la boda de mi primo. Tal vez otro día. Gracias.**

JOAQUÍN **Hola, Roberto. Habla Joaquín. ¿Te gustaría venir a mi casa y ver unos videos?**

ROBERTO **Hombre, gracias. Me gustaría, pero no puedo. Tengo mucha tarea. Tengo que escribir dos composiciones para el lunes. Lo siento.**

18 Anita has been invited to a graduation party, and she's really looking forward to it. Imagine that she's thinking aloud about the party. Write a short paragraph including: what she plans to do at the party, what she does and doesn't feel like doing at the party, and what she has to do to get ready for the party. Use the following verb expressions.

Tengo que · **Quiero** · **Voy a** · **Me gustaría** · **Pienso** · **Necesito** · **Tengo ganas de**

Answers will vary.

■ VAMOS A LEER

19 In the U.S., we tend to take having a phone for granted. However, in some parts of Spain and Latin America, having a telephone in one's home can be the exception rather than the rule. Residents may be put on a long waiting list to have a phone line installed and to get a telephone. Also both local and long-distance calls are extremely expensive. For these reasons, it is not unusual for people in Spanish-speaking countries to use public phone booths or **Telefónicas** *(calling centers)* instead of having a phone at home.

Knowing a little about phones in Spanish-speaking countries can help you understand the reading. Here is a page from a phone book. Look it over, then answer the questions below.

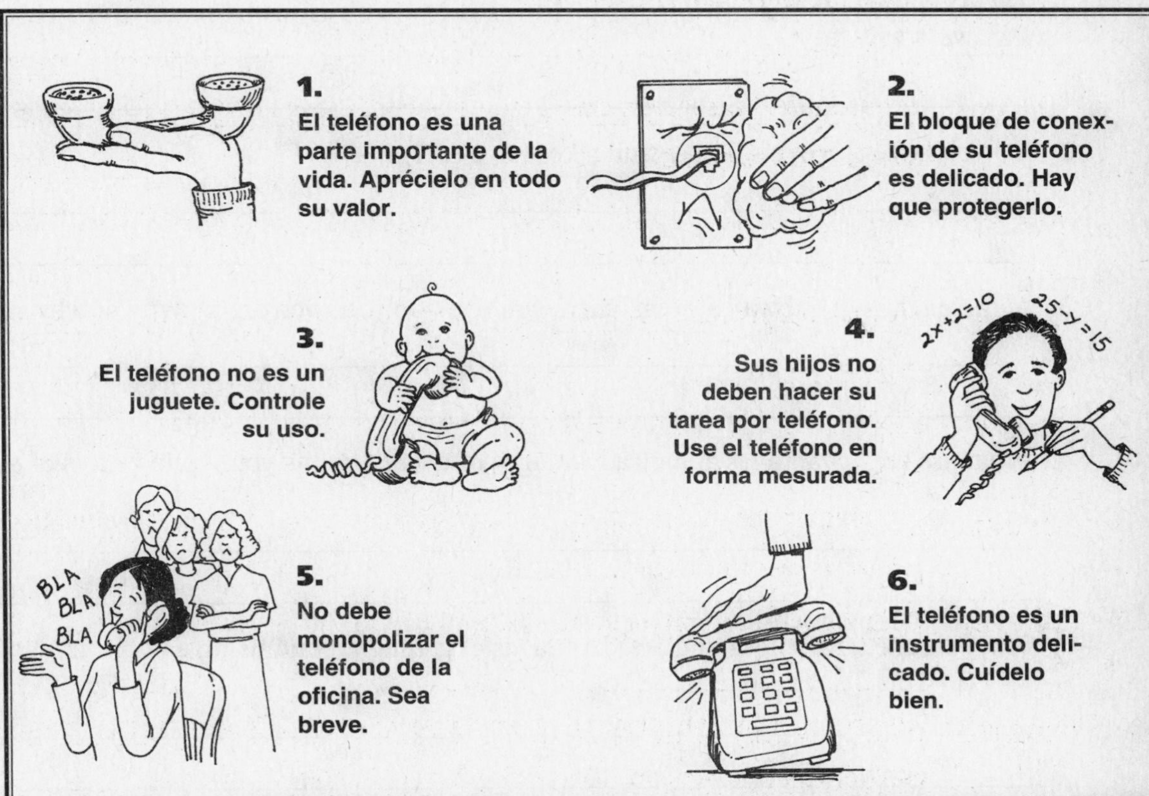

1. What is this information about?
   a. how to get directory assistance
   (b.) how to use phones properly

2. Look at number 3. Based on the drawing, what do you think this rule is saying?
   (a.) phones are not toys
   b. babies can play with the phone as long as no one needs to use it

3. What do numbers 1, 2, and 6 all have in common?
   a. they say that the telephone is part of modern life
   (b.) they urge taking care of the phone and the phone connections

4. Numbers 4 and 5 are also similar. What do they all recommend doing?
   (a.) keeping phone conversations at home and work brief
   b. talking on the phone for a long time at night when the rates are lowest

CULTURA

20 As you read in the **Nota cultural** on p. 189 of your textbook, public transportation is a bigger part of day-to-day life in Spanish-speaking countries than in the U.S. It's not uncommon in larger cities, such as Buenos Aires, Madrid, or Mexico City, for people not to own a car, but to rely instead on the subway or bus systems for transportation. In Spain, the subway is called **el metro**, while in Buenos Aires, it's referred to as **el subte** (short for **el subterráneo**). A public bus in Uruguay and Argentina is **un colectivo** or **un ómnibus**, **una guagua** in Puerto Rico and Cuba, and **un autobús** in Spain. Answer the questions below.

1. How do you generally get to school, to work, and to after-school activities? How do you get around on the weekends?
   Answers will vary.

2. Do you have a driver's license and access to a car?

3. Is there a bus or subway system where you live? Do you ever use it? Why or why not?

4. What are the advantages and disadvantages of using a car as your main means of transportation?

5. What are the advantages and disadvantages of getting around using a public transportation system?

6. Can you imagine living in your area without a car? What would you do instead?

21 Now imagine that you're a student living in Buenos Aires, the capital city of Argentina and you don't have a car. Describe how you get around. What are some advantages and disadvantages?
Answers will vary.

Practice and Activity Book p. 84

VAMOS A LEER

3 A los detalles

1. Linda se arregla a las 7:15.
2. Linda es la última persona que sale de la casa.
3. Le gusta la clase de estudios sociales.
4. Lunes, miércoles y viernes de cinco de la tarde a diez de la noche.
5. A Linda le gustaría estudiar educación.

4 Vamos a comprenderlo bien

1. Porque no le gusta el menú de la cafetería escolar.
2. *Answers will vary.*
3. *Answers will vary.*
4. *Answers will vary.*
5. *Answers will vary.*

5 Reglas de acentuación: las palabras sobresdrújulas

1. anterior
2. c
3. **avísamelo** **diciéndoselo** **cómpramelas** **dándonosla**
   quíteselo **arreglándonoslas** **pasándosela** **apréndetelo**

6 Ortografía: las letras *l, ll* e *y*

1. 1. leyó
   2. hallé
   3. se callaron
   4. estrelló
   5. contribuyó
2. 1. poseyó
   2. falló
   3. huyó
   4. sustituyó
   5. atribuyó
   6. calló
   7. cayó

VAMOS A ESCRIBIR

7 *Answers will vary.*

VAMOS A CONOCERNOS

8 A escuchar

Answers will vary.

9 A pensar

Answers will vary.

10 Así lo decimos nosotros

Se escriben **chiquillo** y **bolillo** con **ll**. Se escribe **haya** con **y**.

Palabra inglesa	Variante local	Español internacional
little boy	chiquío	chiquillo
bread roll	**bolío**	bolillo
to read	leyer	**leer**
apron	delantar	**delantal**
to hear	**oyir**	oír
had	haiga	**haya**
to spell	**espeliar**	deletrear
to eat lunch	lonchar	**almorzar**

VAMOS A CONVERSAR

11 *Answers will vary.*

¡A comer!

RESOURCES

CAPÍTULO 8

¡A comer!

Chapter Teaching Resources Correlation Chart

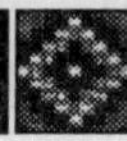

RESOURCES	Print	Audiovisual
De antemano	*Practice and Activity Book*, p. 85	
	Video Guide OR *Videodisc Guide*	*Textbook Audiocassette 4B/Audio CD 8; Video Program* OR *Expanded Video Program, Videocassette 3* OR *Videodisc Program, Videodisc 4B*
Primer paso	*Chapter Teaching Resources, Book 2*	
	• Teaching Transparency Master 8-1, pp. 181, 184	*Teaching Transparency 8-1*
	• Additional Listening Activities 8-1, 8-2, p. 185 —Scripts, p. 212; Answers, p. 214	*Additional Listening Activities, Audiocassette 10A/Audio CD 8*
	• Realia 8-1, pp. 189, 191	
	• Situation Cards 8-1, pp. 192–193	
	• Student Response Forms, p. 194	
	• Quiz 8-1, pp. 197–198 —Scripts, p. 215; Answers, p. 216	*Assessment Items, Audiocassette 8A/Audio CD 8*
	Practice and Activity Book, pp. 86–88 —Answers: *Chapter Teaching Resources, Book 2*, pp. 220–222	
	Native Speaker Activity Book, pp. 36–40 —Answers: *Chapter Teaching Resources, Book 2*, pp. 231–232	
	Videodisc Guide	*Videodisc Program, Videodisc 4B*
	Video Guide	*Video Program* OR *Expanded Video Program, Videocassette 3*
Segundo paso	*Chapter Teaching Resources, Book 2*	
	• Communicative Activity 8-1, pp. 177–178	
	• Teaching Transparency Master 8-2, pp. 182, 184	*Teaching Transparency 8-2*
	• Additional Listening Activities 8-3, 8-4, p. 186 —Scripts, pp. 212–213; Answers, p. 214	*Additional Listening Activities, Audiocassette 10A/Audio CD 8*
	• Realia 8-2, pp. 190, 191	
	• Situation Cards, pp. 192–193	
	• Student Response Form 8-2, p. 195	
	• Quiz 8-2, pp. 199–200 —Scripts, p. 215; Answers, p. 216	*Assessment Items, Audiocassette 8A/Audio CD 8*
	Practice and Activity Book, pp. 89–91 —Answers: *Chapter Teaching Resources, Book 2*, pp. 223–225	
	Native Speaker Activity Book, pp. 36–40 —Answers: *Chapter Teaching Resources, Book 2*, pp. 231–232	
	Videodisc Guide	*Videodisc Program, Videodisc 4B*
Tercer paso	*Chapter Teaching Resources, Book 2*	
	• Communicative Activity 8-2, pp. 179–180	
	• Teaching Transparency Master 8-3, pp. 183, 184	*Teaching Transparency 8-3*
	• Additional Listening Activities 8-5, 8-6, p. 187 —Scripts, p. 213; Answers, p. 214	*Additional Listening Activities, Audiocassette 10A/Audio CD 8*
	• Realia 8-2, pp. 190, 191	
	• Situation Cards 8-3, pp. 192–193	
	• Student Response Form 8-3, p. 196	
	• Quiz 8-3, pp. 201–202 —Scripts, p. 215; Answers, p. 216	*Assessment Items, Audiocassette 8A/Audio CD 8*
	Practice and Activity Book, pp. 92–94 —Answers: *Chapter Teaching Resources, Book 2*, pp. 226–228	
	Native Speaker Activity Book, pp. 36–40 —Answers: *Chapter Teaching Resources, Book 2*, pp. 231–232	
	Videodisc Guide	*Videodisc Program, Videodisc 4B*

ASSESSMENT

Paso Quizzes
- *Chapter Teaching Resources, Book 2*
  Quizzes pp. 197–202
  Scripts and answers pp. 215–216
- Assessment Items, *Audiocassette 8A/Audio CD 8*

Portfolio Assessment
- *Assessment Guide*, pp. 2–13, 21

Chapter Test
- *Chapter Teaching Resources, Book 2*, pp. 203–208
  Test score sheets, pp. 209–210
  Test scripts and answers, pp. 217–218
- *Assessment Guide*, Speaking Test, p. 31
- Assessment Items, *Audiocassette 8A/Audio CD 8*

Test Generator, Chapter 8

Nombre ______________________ Clase ____________ Fecha ____________

Communicative Activity 8-1 A 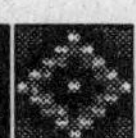

1. You and your partner are planning a lunch for a group of friends. Both of you have been asking around to find out what everyone likes and doesn't like so that you'll know what food to serve. You've spoken to José and Laura and your partner has spoken to Claudia, Martín, and Raúl. Find out from your partner what Claudia, Martín, and Raúl like and don't like.

MODELO — ¿A José qué le gusta?
— Pues, le encanta la sopa de pollo.

	Le encanta(n)	Le gusta(n)	No le gusta(n) para nada
José	la sopa de pollo las manzanas la limonada	el jamón los refrescos	las toronjas la leche
Claudia			
Laura	el queso la piña el café	los perros calientes	el atún
Martín			
Raúl			

2. Now you and your partner need to plan the menu for lunch. Based on what you know about what everybody likes and doesn't like, what are you going to serve?

Pensamos servir	No vamos a servir

CAPÍTULO 8

Nombre ____________________ Clase ____________ Fecha ____________

Communicative Activity 8-1B

1. You and your partner are planning a lunch for a group of friends. Both of you have been asking around to find out what everyone likes and doesn't like so that you'll know what food to serve. You've spoken to Claudia, Martín, and Raúl and your partner has spoken to José and Laura. Find out from your partner what José and Laura like and don't like.

MODELO — ¿A José qué le gusta?
— Pues, le encanta la sopa de pollo.

	Le encanta(n)	**Le gusta(n)**	**No le gusta(n) para nada**
José			
Claudia	el atún la leche	el arroz la limonada los refrescos	las papitas los plátanos
Laura			
Martín	la crema de maní y la jalea	la sopa de pollo	las legumbres
Raúl	el jamón el jugo de naranja	el atún	la crema de maní

2. Now you and your partner need to plan the menu for lunch. Based on what you know about what everybody likes and doesn't like, what are you going to serve?

Pensamos servir	**No vamos a servir**

CAPÍTULO 8

Nombre ______________________ Clase ____________ Fecha ____________

Communicative Activity 8-2A

1. You are a waiter working at an expensive restaurant. Your partner, a customer, would like to order from the daily specials board, but your restaurant lists only the items without their prices. Using the list below, help your customer by answering his or her questions about prices. Use the following model.

MODELO — ¿Qué le puedo traer?
— Quisiera los camarones con bistec, por favor.

Platos del día	
• bocadillo de jamón con papas fritas	5500
• pescado con arroz y legumbres	6100
Entremeses	
• ensalada mixta	2000
• ensalada de atún	2100
Bebidas	
• agua mineral	600
• café	800
• café con leche	850
• soda	850
Postres	
• helado	1500
• pastel de chocolate	1800

2. Now it's your turn to role-play the customer. Your partner, the waiter, will tell you the prices on the daily specials board. You only have 3000 **pesetas** to spend. Write the prices next to the items on the list below. Then decide what you will order and how much to tip the waiter.

Platos del día

arroz con pollo ____________

camarones con bistec ____________

Entremeses

frijoles ____________

legumbres ____________

Postres

helado ____________

pastel de chocolate ____________

Bebidas

jugo de naranja ____________

café ____________

café con leche ____________

soda ____________

Voy a pedir ______________________ y ______________________.

Y para tomar, quisiera ______________________.

De propina voy a dejar ______________________.

CAPÍTULO 8

Nombre ______________________ Clase ____________ Fecha ____________

Communicative Activity 8-2B

1. You are a customer at an expensive restaurant. Your partner, the waiter, will tell you the prices on the daily specials board. You only have 3000 **pesetas** to spend. Write the prices next to the items on the list below. Then decide what you will order, and how much to tip the waiter.

Platos del día

bocadillo de jamón con papas fritas ____________

pescado con arroz y legumbres ____________

Entremeses

ensalada mixta ____________

ensalada de atún ____________

Postres

helado ____________

pastel de chocolate ____________

Bebidas

agua mineral ____________

café ____________

café con leche ____________

soda ____________

Voy a pedir ______________________ y ______________________.

Y para tomar, quisiera ______________________.

De propina voy a dejar ______________________.

2. Now it's your turn to play the waiter. Your partner, a customer, would like to order from the daily specials board, but your restaurant lists only the items without their prices. Using the list below, help your customer by answering his or her questions about prices. Use the following model.

MODELO — ¿Qué le puedo traer?
— Quisiera el pescado con arroz y legumbres, por favor.

Platos del día	
• arroz con pollo	6500
• camarones con bistec	8700
Entremeses	
• frijoles	1800
• legumbres	1900
Bebidas	
• jugo de naranja	750
• café	700
• café con leche	800
• soda	850
Postres	
• helado	1200
• pastel de chocolate	1750

Nombre ______________________ Clase ______________ Fecha ______________

Teaching Transparency Master 8-1

CAPÍTULO 8

Nombre ______________________ Clase ______________ Fecha ______________

Teaching Transparency Master 8-2

Nombre ______________________ Clase ______________ Fecha ______________

Teaching Transparency Master 8-3

Using Teaching Transparencies 8-1, 8-2, 8-3

Teaching Transparency 8-1

1. **Listening:** Say what people are eating and ask students to identify the meal.
   MODELO — **Ellos comen huevos, tocino, pan tostado...**
   — **El desayuno.**
2. **Speaking:** Point to a person in one of the scenes and ask students to make up a name for him or her. Then ask the student to say what he or she is eating.
   MODELO — **¿Cómo se llama ella?**
   — **Se llama Elena.**
   — **¿Qué come Elena?**
   — **Come...**
3. **Pair work/Speaking/Writing:** Have students interview one another about their own typical breakfasts or lunches and write the information in a list. Then ask a few students to report to the class.

Teaching Transparency 8-2

1. **Listening:** Imagine that you're one of the people and talk about your meal. Have the students identify the person and what he or she is eating.
   MODELO — **¡Ay, están demasiado picantes!**
   — **El muchacho que come la comida mexicana.**
2. **Listening/Speaking:** Make a statement about one of the people's reaction to his or her food. Have students say whether your statement is **cierto** or **falso**. If it's false, have them correct it.
   MODELO — **A este muchacho no le gusta la pizza para nada.**
   — **Falso. A él le encanta.**
3. **Pair work/Speaking:** Have students do Activity 1 with a partner.
4. **Speaking:** Have students talk about the food in their high school cafeteria.
5. **Writing:** Have students write a short paragraph describing the scene. Have them include the following elements: the location, time of day, physical description of the people, description of the meals being eaten, and how the people feel about their meals.

Teaching Transparency 8-3

1. **Listening:** Describe some of the problems the people in the restaurant are experiencing and have students identify whom you are describing.
   MODELO — **No puedo comer el pastel porque no tengo tenedor.**
   — **El hombre.**
2. **Listening:** Take the role of one of the people in the restaurant and ask the waiter for the item that you need. Then ask the students to identify who you are.
   MODELO — **Camarero, ¿nos puede traer un menú?**
   — **Uno de los muchachos que no tiene menú.**
3. **Pair work/Speaking:** Have students role-play a conversation between the waiter and someone else in the transparency.
4. **Writing:** Have students write a menu of their own.

Nombre ______________________ Clase ______________ Fecha ______________

 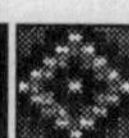

PRIMER PASO

8-1 Listen as several students talk about what they eat for breakfast. Write the person's name below what he or she eats.

______________ ______________ ______________ ______________

______________ ______________ ______________

8-2 Today is Laura's turn to pick up lunch for the people at work. Listen as everyone tells her what they want, and complete each person's order below.

Nombre	Comida	Bebida
Antonia	una sopa de legumbres; una __________ de lechuga y __________	un vaso de __________
Lucía	__________________ ; unas papitas	una limonada grande
Carlos	un sándwich de __________________; __________________ una ensalada de __________________	un __________________
Sra. Mercado	una __________________	un té frío

Nombre ______________________ Clase ______________ Fecha ______________

Additional Listening Activities

SEGUNDO PASO

8-3 You overhear several conversations in a crowded restaurant. Listen to each one and decide if each person likes his or her food.

1. Rafa sí no
2. Mónica sí no
3. Ernesto sí no
4. Nuria sí no
5. Horacio sí no
6. Beatriz sí no

8-4 It's Saturday morning and Sr. Sánchez is getting ready to go to the supermarket. Listen to Sr. and Sra. Sánchez talk about what they need to buy. Make a list of the groceries they decide upon.

____

____

____

____

____

____

TERCER PASO

8-5 Listen to these conversations and answer the following questions based on what you hear.

1. La muchacha necesita otro ______.
   a. sándwich
   b. tenedor

2. Al muchacho le encanta ______.
   a. el flan
   b. el helado

3. Esta persona va a ______.
   a. pedir el plato del día porque le encantan los camarones
   b. pedir una cena ligera porque no tiene mucha hambre

4. Este señor quiere ______.
   a. pagar la cuenta
   b. atún con cebolla y tomate

8-6 In family-owned restaurants, it's not uncommon for waiters to tell customers the amount of the bill instead of giving them a written bill. Listen as José María adds up the totals for different customers, and write the correct total for each one.

Nombre ______________________ Clase __________ Fecha __________

Additional Listening Activities

SONG

In Mexico an owl is called a **tecolote**. This song is from the state of Michoacán, where in the forests one can hear the songs of many different birds, among them **el tecolote**.

El tecolote

Tecolote de guadaña,
Pájaro madrugador. *(Repite)*
¿Me prestarás tus alitas,
Me prestarás tus alitas,
Me prestarás tus alitas
Para ir a ver a mi amor,
Para ir a ver a mi amor?

Ticuri cuiri, cuiri, cu
Ticuri cuiri, cuiri, cu
Ticuri cuiri, cuiri, cu.
Pobrecito tecolote,
Ya se cansa de volar.

This song is recorded on *Audio CD 8* and also on *Audiocassette 11: Songs.* Although it is presented with this chapter, it can be used at any time.

Nombre ______________________ Clase ____________ Fecha ____________

Realia 8-1

ZUMO EL ANDALUZ
1 lt.
75

EL ANDALUZ ZUMO

CROQUETAS TÍA ISABEL
500 grs.
175

CROQUETAS TIA ISABEL

Pizza Napoli

PIZZAS NAPOLI
Tamaño mediano
175

POLLO ENTERO, kg.
189

Huevos Categoría Extra
docena, 60/65 grs.
138

MARGARINA Clavel 500 grs.

Margarina Clavel
500 grs.
119

DEL CAMPO
16 LONCHAS DE QUESO

Queso Del Campo,
16 lonchas
175

FRUTAS Y VERDURAS

Manzanas Rojas Granel	Patatas	Plátanos	Uvas 1ª
110 pts./kg.	13 pts./kg.	145 pts./kg.	95 pts./kg.

CAPÍTULO 8

Realia 8-2

No. DE SERVICIOS	CUARTO	CUBIERTOS	FECHA	MESERO

DESAYUNO CONTINENTAL

___ $10,500 JUGO NARANJA ___ TORONJA ___ TOMATE ___
PAN DULCE ___ PAN TOSTADO ___ MANTEQUILLA
MERMELADA ___ CAFE ___ TE ___ LECHE ___

DESAYUNO A LA CARTA

___ $5,000 JUGO DE NARANJA TORONJA TOMATE
___ $5,500 PLATO DE FRUTAS TROPICALES
___ $12,000 HUEVOS FRITOS TIBIOS REVUELTOS
___ $12,000 RANCHEROS A LA MEXICANA
___ $12,500 MOTULEÑOS
___ $7,000 ORDEN DE JAMON ___ TOCINO ___ SALCHICHA ___
___ $5,000 HOT CAKES CON MIEL

CEREALES

___ $5,500 AMPLIO SURTIDO DE CEREALES ACOMPAÑADOS CON FRUTAS DE LA TEMPORADA ___

BEBIDAS

___ $3,500 CAFE
___ $3,300 TE
___ $3,200 LECHE
___ $4,000 JUGO
___ $3,500 CHOCOLATE

NO SE SERVIRÁ SI NO LLEVA SU FIRMA
NOMBRE
FIRMA ______________________

CAPÍTULO 8

Realia 8-1 : Supermarket advertisement

1. **Reading:** Have students look over the ad and then ask them what kind of store is being advertised. Point out the words **zumo**, **patata**, and the abbreviation **pts**. Then ask students what country they think this ad comes from.

2. **Listening:** Prepare a list of some common foods. Include some of the foods that are in the ad and some that aren't. Read your list aloud and ask students to say whether each item you mention is advertised or not.

3. **Listening:** Name the price of some items and have students identify the item by name.

4. **Writing:** Have students prepare a grocery list based on the ad. Then ask them to write a meal they can prepare with the groceries. Tell students to include three items they might also need that are not in the ad.

5. **Pair work/Speaking:** Have students work in pairs and have them tell each other what they're going to buy. Ask students to report their partner's choices to the class.

Realia 8-2: Room service menu

1. **Reading:** Have students read over the menu, and then ask them what type of restaurant uses this kind of menu. Then ask students what meal can be ordered from this menu.

2. **Pair work/Reading:** Have students work in pairs. Ask them to use context to guess unfamiliar words and phrases such as **salchicha, mantequilla, mermelada, frutas de la temporada,** and **No se servirá si no lleva su firma.**

3. **Listening:** Imagine that you're ordering over the phone and have students take your order.

4. **Pair work/Speaking:** Have students work in pairs and take each other's orders. The student who takes the order should also add up the bill and then tell his or her partner the total.

5. **Group work/Writing:** Have students work in groups to create their own room service menus.

Nombre ______________________ Clase ______________ Fecha ______________

Situation Cards 8-1, 8-2, 8-3: Interview

Situation 8-1 : Interview

Imagine I'm an exchange student new to the United States. Answer my questions about food and meals.

¿Qué comes en el desayuno?
¿Quién prepara los desayunos en tu familia?
¿A qué hora almuerzas?
¿En qué consiste un almuerzo típico en los Estados Unidos?

Situation 8-2: Interview

Imagine you work at a cafeteria and I come through the line with the following questions about the food. How would you respond?

¿Están muy picantes los frijoles?
¿Cómo está el postre hoy?
¿Qué frutas hay hoy?
¿Qué sándwiches hay?

Situation 8-3: Interview

Imagine I'm a customer in a restaurant and you're the wait-person. How would you respond?

Camarero/a, ¿me puede traer el menú, por favor?
Camarero/a, este tenedor está sucio.
¿Me puede traer la cuenta?
¿Está incluida la propina?

Situation Cards 8-1, 8-2, 8-3: Role-playing

Situation 8-1: Role-playing

Student A Imagine you like a light breakfast and **Student B** likes a heavy one. Tell **Student B** your opinion and include what you typically eat. Then ask **Student B** what he or she eats for breakfast.

Student B **Student A** doesn't eat much and you like to eat a lot for breakfast! Listen to what **Student A** says about his or her typical breakfast. Then answer **Student A**'s question. Include at least five different items that you enjoy eating for breakfast.

ligero fuerte el cereal los huevos típicamente

Situation 8-2: Role-playing

Student A Imagine that you and **Student B** are eating dinner at a restaurant. **Student B** asks you several questions about how your food tastes. Let **Student B** know if the foods taste salty, cold, hot, or delicious.

Student B Imagine that you and **Student A** are eating dinner at a restaurant. Ask **Student A** how the following items taste: the soup, the chicken, the vegetables, and the dessert.

¿Cómo está(n)? salado rico caliente frío
el pollo el postre la sopa las legumbres

Situation 8-3: Role-playing

Student A Imagine that you're a waitperson and **Student B** is your customer. Ask **Student B** if he or she wants dessert. Then bring **Student B** the bill. Tell him or her how much it is and that the tip isn't included.

Student B You have just finished your meal at a restaurant and **Student B** is your waitperson. Answer **Student A**'s question and tell him or her what you want for dessert. After ordering dessert, ask **Student A** for the bill. Then ask **Student A** if the tip is included.

postre ¿Está incluida la propina? Quisiera pedir...

Nombre ______________________ Clase ____________ Fecha ____________

Student Response Forms

6 Escuchemos: El desayuno p. 208

Listen as Marcela and Roberto discuss what foods they like and dislike. Write what each person likes for breakfast.

Marcela	Roberto
____________	____________
____________	____________
____________	____________
____________	____________

12 Escuchemos: ¿Cómo es la comida aquí? p. 210

Listen as an Ecuadorean student asks about meals in the United States. Write the time her friend says he eats each meal in the U.S., and what he eats.

El desayuno:

Hora: ____________

Come: ____________

El almuerzo:

Hora: ____________

Come: ____________

16 Escuchemos: Comentarios p. 212

Listen as some customers comment on the food at **El Rincón**, a restaurant. Write the food item each person mentions. Then, if the person likes the food, write **sí.** If not, write **no.**

1. ____________
2. ____________
3. ____________
4. ____________
5. ____________
6. ____________

CAPÍTULO 8

21 Escuchemos: En el restaurante p. 213

Cuatro amigos están en un café popular. Escucha mientras hablan de lo que van a comer. Luego contesta estas preguntas.

1. ¿Quién quiere desayunar? ______________________
2. ¿Quién tiene sed? ______________________
3. ¿Quién no tiene hambre? ______________________
4. ¿Quién va a comer sopa? ______________________
5. ¿Qué hay para el desayuno? ______________________

28 Escuchemos: Me trae... p. 217

Imagine you're eating at **Restaurante El Molino**, a busy restaurant in Quito. Listen to these orders and decide if each person is ordering breakfast, lunch, dinner, or dessert. Then place a check mark in the appropriate column.

	Breakfast	Lunch	Dinner	Dessert
1.				
2.				
3.				
4.				
5.				
6.				
7.				
8.				

Nombre ______________________ Clase ____________ Fecha ____________

Student Response Forms

32 Escuchemos: ¿Cuánto es? p. 219

Look at the menu and listen to the following prices. Match the price mentioned with the correct item on the menu.

_____ 1.
_____ 2.
_____ 3.
_____ 4.
_____ 5.
_____ 6.

a. Ensalada mixta 5.500
b. Ceviche de camarón 8.500
c. Sancocho 7.000
d. Pollo al ajillo 8.750
e. Plato vegetariano 6.300
f. Agua de Güitig 2.000
g. Té frío 1.500
h. Helado de naranjilla 4.000
i. Canoa de frutas 4.500

Repaso Activity 1: p. 224

Listen as Ángel talks about some foods he likes and doesn't like. Write the foods Ángel mentions in the correct columns.

Ángel likes	Ángel doesn't like
____________	____________
____________	____________
____________	____________

CAPÍTULO 8

CAPÍTULO 8

Nombre ______________________ Clase ____________ Fecha ____________

¡A comer!

Quiz 8-1

PRIMER PASO

Maximum Score: 35

I. Listening

A. Listen as Luisa and Roberto talk about what they like to eat for breakfast. As they say what they like, place a check mark in the appropriate box. Not everything they mention is listed here. (10 points)

	Luisa	Roberto
1. huevos		
2. jugo de naranja		
3. leche		
4. pan tostado		
5. tocino		

SCORE ______

II. Reading

B. Marilú likes to go to El Rinconcito Restaurant with Manuel. Complete her conversation by choosing the correct word for each blank from the word box. Not all the words will be used. (10 points)

ocupadas	nos	almuerzan	le	almuerzo
almorzamos	me	para nada	te	

Manuel y yo siempre 6. ______________ a la una. A veces comemos un sándwich, pero también 7. ______________ encanta la sopa de queso. No nos gusta la sopa de legumbres 8. ______________. Y tú, ¿qué 9. ______________ encanta comer para el 10. ______________?

SCORE ______

CAPÍTULO 8

Quiz 8-1

III. Writing

C. Write five sentences describing what you normally have for breakfast and lunch: one sentence each for what you eat for breakfast and lunch; one sentence each for what you drink with breakfast and lunch; one sentence naming a food or drink that you especially love. (10 points)

11. ______________________________

12. ______________________________

13. ______________________________

14. ______________________________

15. ______________________________

SCORE [ ]

IV. Culture

D. Based on the information in your book, answer **a) cierto** or **b) falso** to the following statements. (5 points)

____ 16. In Spanish-speaking countries, a breakfast consisting of a roll, fresh fruit, and hot chocolate would be rather unusual.

____ 17. Lunch in Spanish-speaking countries is a light meal consisting of soup or a sandwich.

SCORE [ ]

TOTAL SCORE [/35]

Nombre ____________________ Clase __________ Fecha __________

CAPÍTULO 8

¡A comer!

Quiz 8-3

TERCER PASO

Maximum Score: 35

I. Listening

A. Rosita is working as a waitress in a restaurant. The people at the table she's waiting on right now want to know the prices of various items. As Rosita answers, write the price for each item. (10 points)

	COMIDA	PRECIO
1.		______________ sucres
2.		______________ sucres
3.		______________ sucres
4.		______________ sucres
5.		______________ sucres

SCORE [ ]

II. Reading

B. The restaurant you're in is so noisy that you and the waitperson keep hearing what's said at other tables. Show what you and the waitperson really say to each other by choosing the right letter. (10 points)

_____ **6.** ¿Qué le puedo traer?
a. Primero quisiera la ensalada de fruta.
b. Es aparte. No está incluida.

_____ **7.** Camarera, hay una mosca *(fly)* en el té.
¿Me trae otro vaso, por favor?
a. ¡Claro que sí!
b. ¿Cuánto es?

_____ **8.** ¿Qué legumbre quiere?
a. La cuenta, por favor.
b. El maíz, por favor.

CAPÍTULO 8

Nombre ______________________ Clase ______________ Fecha ______________

Quiz 8-3

______ 9. ¿Desea algo más?
  a. ¿Es aparte la propina?
  b. Quisiera un postre, por favor.

______ 10. La cuenta, por favor.
  a. Muy bien. La propina está incluida.
  b. Prefiero la sopa del día.

SCORE

III. Writing

C. The waitperson is taking your order. Write five sentences to complete the following. (10 points)

CAMARERA ¿Qué le puedo traer?

11. TÚ ______________________

CAMARERA ¿Y qué legumbres quiere?

12. TÚ ______________________

CAMARERA ¿Quiere una ensalada?

13. TÚ ______________________

CAMARERA Y para tomar, ¿prefiere té o un refresco?

14. TÚ ______________________

CAMARERA ¿Algo más?

15. TÚ ______________________

SCORE

IV. Culture

D. Based on the information in your book, answer **a) cierto** or **b) falso** to the following statements. (5 points)

______ 16. Many people in Spanish-speaking countries do not switch the fork to the right hand after cutting food.

______ 17. In Spain, a **tortilla** is made from cormeal or flour, pressed into a flat shape and cooked on a griddle.

SCORE

TOTAL SCORE /35

CUMULATIVE SCORE FOR QUIZZES 1–3 /100

Nombre ______________________ Clase ____________ Fecha ____________

¡A comer!

Chapter 8 Test

I. Listening

Maximum Score: 30 points

A. Listen as a group of friends talk about what they want for lunch. Match each person with what he or she says. (8 points)

1. ______
2. ______
3. ______
4. ______

a. Lupe
b. Sebastián
c. Victoria
d. Héctor

SCORE

B. Carmiña and Miguel have gone to a restaurant for dinner. Listen to the conversation between them and their waiter. Then indicate what each of them had to eat by putting **a)** for **Carmiña**, **b)** for **Miguel**, or **c)** for **neither** next to the food item. (22 points)

______ **5.** arroz con pollo
______ **6.** pastel
______ **7.** café
______ **8.** carne de res
______ **9.** flan
______ **10.** helado de chocolate
______ **11.** leche
______ **12.** té frío
______ **13.** un sándwich
______ **14.** camarones
______ **15.** sopa

SCORE

CAPÍTULO 8

Chapter 8 Test

II. Reading

Maximum Score: 30 points

C. Carlos is writing about his trip to a restaurant. Read his story and answer the questions which follow it. (10 points)

Hoy estamos en el restaurante "La Margarita". Son las doce y media y estoy con mis amigos José, Carmen, Luisa y Juan Luis. Nos gusta mucho salir y comer en los restaurantes de la ciudad. Carmen dice que la comida aquí siempre es muy rica. Hoy tienen muchos platos deliciosos. Hay también una camarera muy amable. La mesa es muy grande, cerca de la puerta. A mí me encanta la comida española.

La camarera nos trae el menú y nos pregunta qué vamos a pedir. Las chicas quieren una ensalada fresca porque hace mucho calor. La ensalada tiene uvas, toronjas y naranjas. ¡Qué rica! Juan Luis pide jamón con legumbres y José pide sopa de cebolla. Yo quiero la carne de res con arroz y maíz. De postre las chicas y José no quieren nada, pero yo como pastel de chocolate y a Juan Luis le gusta el flan. Después del postre, tomamos café, pagamos la cuenta y salimos a pasear.

_____ **16.** Los chicos tienen una mesa para...
- **a.** desayunar
- **b.** almorzar
- **c.** cenar

_____ **17.** La comida del restaurante es muy...
- **a.** buena
- **b.** mala
- **c.** salada

_____ **18.** Las chicas prefieren algo...
- **a.** ligero
- **b.** caliente
- **c.** picante

_____ **19.** De postre, Carlos pide...
- **a.** pastel
- **b.** flan
- **c.** café

_____ **20.** Los chicos pagan cuando la camarera trae...
- **a.** la propina
- **b.** la cuenta
- **c.** el flan

SCORE

D. Read the following ad for **Fonda del mar**. Then answer the questions that follow. (6 points)

Fonda del mar

Pescado y mariscos (*shellfish*) para usted y para toda su familia. Los preparamos frescos todos los días.

Escuche lo que dicen nuestros clientes:

Carlota Méndez: En Fonda del mar la comida está riquísima. Sirven de todos los mariscos: camarones, langostas, mejillas, almejas y ostras. Y los sirven rápido y calientes como en su casa.

Paco Cárdenas: En otros restaurantes los mariscos salen muy salados. En Fonda del mar, los cocineros se dedican mucho a sus platos. Siempre están perfectos los mariscos y nunca salados.

María Saavedra: A mí me encanta la comida picante. En Fonda del mar tienen platos especiales para mí. Si a usted le gusta la comida picante, ¡venga a comer en Fonda del mar!

Carlitos Saavedra: De postre, me encanta el flan.

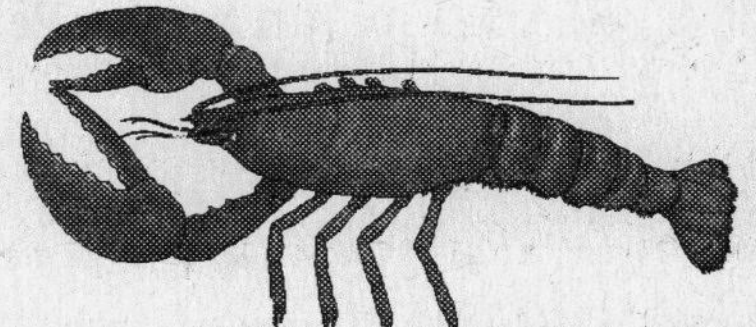

Fonda del mar
19402 avenida de la iglesia
tel: 54-34-92-95

_____ 21. What is **Fonda del mar**?
a. a restaurant supply store
b. a wholesale seafood store
c. a restaurant

_____ 22. What does Paco Cárdenas give as his main complaint about shellfish at some restaurants?
a. They're too hot.
b. They're too cold.
c. They're too salty.

_____ 23. What kind of food does María Saavedra like?
a. spicy food
b. cold food
c. salads

SCORE ______

Chapter 8 Test

E. Carlos and Adela are ordering lunch at a restaurant. Complete their conversation with the words from the word bank. Use each word only once. (14 points)

trae	cuenta	me	hambre	le
nos	almuerzo	otra		

ADELA Me gustaría pedir los camarones, por favor.

CARLOS Yo no tengo mucha **24.** __________. Por lo general, **25.** __________ a las dos. Quiero algo ligero.

CAMARERO Pues, señor, tenemos algunas ensaladas buenísimas hoy. ¿Le gustaría una?

CARLOS Claro. ¿Me **26.** __________ una de frutas frescas, por favor? Y un café.

CAMARERO Está bien. ¿Y Ud., señorita? ¿Desea algo para beber?

ADELA Sí, para mí, un té frío. Perdón, señor, pero necesito **27.** __________ cuchara. Esta cuchara está sucia.

CAMARERO Ahora mismo. ¿**28.** __________ gustaría un postre?

CARLOS No, gracias. **29.** __________ encantan los postres, pero estoy a dieta.

CAMARERO ¿Y Ud., señorita?

ADELA Sí, por favor. ¿Me puede traer una galletas y después la **30.** __________?

SCORE ☐

III. Culture

Maximum Score: 8 points

F. Read the statements below. Based on the information in your textbook, determine whether the statements are **a) cierto** or **b) falso**. (8 points)

_____ **31.** Spaniards brought turkey and chocolate to the Americas when they came.

_____ **32.** Most Ecuadorean food is not very spicy.

_____ **33.** **Una merienda** is a heavy meal eaten around 8:00 P.M.

_____ **34.** The "typical dish" in Spain and Latin America varies from country to country.

SCORE ☐

CAPÍTULO 8

IV. Writing

Maximum Score: 32 points

G. Write a conversation between the waiter and Carolina in which you include the following: (12 points)

- The waiter asks Carolina how the soup is.
- Carolina says she doesn't like the soup at all.
- The waiter asks Carolina why she doesn't like the soup.
- Carolina says that the soup is cold and salty.
- The waiter asks if he can bring her anything else.
- Carolina says no thank you.

35. CAMARERO ______________________________

____

36. CAROLINA ______________________________

____

37. CAMARERO ______________________________

____

38. CAROLINA ______________________________

____

39. CAMARERO ______________________________

____

40. CAROLINA ______________________________

____

SCORE [ ]

Nombre ______________________ Clase ____________ Fecha ____________

Chapter 8 Test

H. Describe your favorite meal of the day. Explain what foods you like to eat and what you like about each one. (10 points)

41. ____

SCORE

I. You and your friend have just finished eating in an Ecuadorean restaurant. You now need to pay the bill in **sucres** (*Ecuadorean money*). Write five sentences in Spanish for the following situation. (10 points)

a. Your friend asks for the bill.

b. You ask your friend how much the bill is.

c. Your friend says it's 22.240 **sucres**. (Write the number as words.)

d. You ask if the tip is included.

e. Your friend says it's separate. It's 3.300 **sucres**. (Write the number as words.)

42. TU AMIGO ____

43. TÚ ____

44. TU AMIGO ____

45. TÚ ____

46. TU AMIGO ____

SCORE

TOTAL SCORE /100

CAPÍTULO 8

Nombre ______________________ Clase ____________ Fecha ____________

CAPÍTULO 8 Chapter Test Score Sheet

Circle the letter that matches the most appropriate response.

I. Listening

Maximum Score: 30 points

A. (8 points)

1. a b c d
2. a b c d
3. a b c d
4. a b c d

SCORE ☐

B. (22 points)

5. a b
6. a b
7. a b
8. a b
9. a b
10. a b
11. a b
12. a b
13. a b
14. a b
15. a b

SCORE ☐

II. Reading

Maximum Score: 30 points

C. (10 points)

16. a b c
17. a b c
18. a b c
19. a b c
20. a b c

SCORE ☐

D. (6 points)

21. a b c
22. a b c
23. a b c

SCORE ☐

E. (14 points)

24. ______________
25. ______________
26. ______________
27. ______________
28. ______________
29. ______________
30. ______________

SCORE ☐

III. Culture

Maximum Score: 10 points

F. (8 points)

31. a b
32. a b
33. a b
34. a b

SCORE ☐

Nombre ______________________ Clase ____________ Fecha ____________

IV. Writing

Maximum Score: 32 points

G. (12 points)

35. CAMARERO ______________________

36. CAROLINA ______________________

37. CAMARERO ______________________

38. CAROLINA ______________________

39. CAMARERO ______________________

40. CAROLINA ______________________

SCORE

H. (10 points)

41. ______________________

SCORE

I. (10 points)

42. ______________________

43. ______________________

44. ______________________

45. ______________________

46. ______________________

SCORE

TOTAL SCORE /100

CAPÍTULO 8

RESOURCES

Scripts and Answers

Additional Listening Activity 8-1, p.185

MARTA Hola. Me llamo Marta. Por lo general tomo un vaso de jugo de naranja y como un poco de pan tostado con jalea.
PEDRO Me llamo Pedro. No me gustan los desayunos fuertes. Para el desayuno, tomo un vaso de leche y preparo una ensalada de frutas con uvas y plátanos.
SUSANA Me llamo Susana. Por las mañanas no como mucho. Sólo un poco de cereal.
RAMÓN Hola. Soy Ramón. En mi casa siempre desayunamos mucho. Generalmente, como tres huevos fritos con tocino y pan dulce. ¡El desayuno es delicioso!

Additional Listening Activity 8-2, p.185

LAURA Antonia, ¿qué quieres para el almuerzo hoy?
ANTONIA Mmm... quiero una sopa de legumbres, por favor.
LAURA ¿Eso es todo?
ANTONIA No... también quiero una ensalada de lechuga y tomate. Y de tomar, un vaso de leche.
LAURA Perfecto.

LAURA Lucía, ¿qué quieres para el almuerzo?
LUCÍA A ver... pues, tengo ganas de comer uno... no, dos... dos perros calientes. Y unas papitas también, por favor.
LAURA Bueno. ¿Qué quieres para tomar?
LUCÍA Una limonada grande.
LAURA Muy bien.

LAURA Oye, Carlos, ¿qué quieres para el almuerzo?
CARLOS Pues, un sándwich de jamón y queso. Y también una ensalada de frutas, por favor.
LAURA ¿Quieres algo de tomar?
CARLOS Sí, un café grande, por favor.

LAURA Sra. Mercado, perdone que la interrumpa. Voy al café a comprar el almuerzo. ¿Quiere Ud. algo?
SRA. MERCADO Sí, déjame pensar... pues, tráeme una sopa de pollo, por favor.
LAURA ¿No quiere nada más?
SRA. MERCADO No, sólo la sopa, gracias. No tengo mucha hambre. Y de tomar, quisiera un té frío, por favor.
LAURA Muy bien.
SRA. MERCADO Gracias, Laura.
LAURA De nada.

Additional Listening Activity 8-3, p.186

ANITA Rafa, ¿cómo está la sopa?
RAFA ¡Uy! Está horrible. Está salada y fría.

GUILLERMO Mónica, ¿cómo están las enchiladas?
MÓNICA Riquísimas. Me encantan las enchiladas de queso. ¿Quieres probarlas?

HILDA Ernesto, ¿qué es eso? ¿Qué estás comiendo?
ERNESTO Es una pizza de atún y piña. ¡Es mi pizza favorita! Me encanta.

JAVIER Nuria, no estás comiendo nada. ¿No te gusta el pollo?
NURIA Está muy picante, y a mí no me gusta mucho la comida picante.
JAVIER ¿Por qué no pides otra cosa?

MERCEDES Horacio, ¿cómo están las empanadas?
HORACIO Están bien ricas. Las de carne son muy buenas, pero las de pollo son deliciosas. Creo que voy a pedir unas más.

PEDRO Beatriz, ¿cómo está el sándwich?
BEATRIZ Pues, el sándwich tiene mucho pan y mucha lechuga... ¡pero no tiene nada de jamón ni de queso! Voy a hablar con el camarero ahora. ¡Camarero!

Additional Listening Activity 8-4, p.186

SR. SÁNCHEZ Querida, voy a salir dentro de un rato para hacer compras. ¿Debemos hacer una lista?
SRA. SÁNCHEZ Sí. ¿Qué tenemos que comprar?
SR. SÁNCHEZ A ver... necesitamos café... y necesitamos frijoles.
SRA. SÁNCHEZ Bueno... ¿por qué no compras un poco de fruta? Ya tenemos naranjas en casa, pero me gustaría comprar unas fresas. Los batidos de leche, plátano y fresas son ricos siempre.
SR. SÁNCHEZ De acuerdo. A los niños les encantan.
SRA. SÁNCHEZ A propósito, los niños quieren hamburguesas esta noche. ¿Qué te parece? Si tú también quieres hamburguesas, necesitas comprar carne de res.
SR. SÁNCHEZ Está bien. ¿Quieres lechuga también?
SRA. SÁNCHEZ No, no creo. Ya tenemos lechuga.
SR. SÁNCHEZ ¿Qué más?
SRA. SÁNCHEZ Déjame pensar. De postre, voy a hacer un flan. Necesito huevos y leche.
SR. SÁNCHEZ Bueno, si no necesitamos más, me voy. Hasta luego.
SRA. SÁNCHEZ Hasta pronto.

Additional Listening Activity 8-5, p.187

LUPE Oiga, camarero, este tenedor está sucio. ¿Me puede traer otro?
CAMARERO Cómo no. Se lo traigo enseguida

GERMÁN Camarero, la cuenta, por favor.
CAMARERO ¿Desea algo más?
GERMÁN Bueno, tal vez un poco de flan, gracias. Me encanta el flan.
CAMARERO Muy bien.

CAMARERO Muy buenas noches. ¿Qué le puedo traer? Hoy el plato del día es camarones al mojo de ajo. Están riquísimos esta noche.
FERNANDA Bueno, es que no tengo mucha hambre. Quisiera sopa de pollo y un batido de fresa.
CAMARERO Excelente.

CAMARERO Son tres mil quinientos sucres, señor.
SANTI Muy bien. ¿Está incluida la propina?
CAMARERO No, es aparte.

Additional Listening Activity 8-6, p.187

JOSÉ MARÍA Pues... son dos platos del día a mil doscientos cada uno... más dos limonadas y una botella de agua mineral... a ver... en total, son tres mil pesetas.
JOSÉ MARÍA Vamos a ver... dos ensaladas de frutas, un bistec, un pescado con almendras y dos batidos... Son dos mil cincuenta pesetas, muchachos.
JOSÉ MARÍA A ver... dos cafés y un flan... Son ochocientas pesetas, señores.
JOSÉ MARÍA Pues... un sándwich de jamón, una ensalada de atún, una de frutas, una sopa de pollo y cuatro de té frío... Son dos mil setecientas pesetas, muchachas.

Answers to Additional Listening Activities

Additional Listening Activity 8-1, p.185

Marta—jugo de naranja, pan tostado
Pedro—leche, ensalada de frutas
Susana—ceréal
Ramón—huevos con tocino, pan dulce

Additional Listening Activity 8-2, p.185

Nombre	Comida	Bebida
Antonia	una sopa de legumbres; una **ensalada** de lechuga y **tomate**	un vaso de **leche**
Lucía	**dos perros calientes**; unas papitas	una limonada grande
Carlos	un sándwich de **jamón y queso**; ______ una ensalada de **frutas**	un **café grande**
Sra. Mercado	una **sopa de pollo**	un té frío

Additional Listening Activity 8-3, p.186

1. no
2. sí
3. sí
4. no
5. sí
6. no

Additional Listening Activity 8-4, p.186

café
frijoles
fresas
carne de res
huevos
leche

Additional Listening Activity 8-5, p.187

1. b 2. a 3. b 4. a

Additional Listening Activity 8-6, p.187

1. 3.000 ptas.
2. 2.050 ptas.
3. 800 ptas.
4. 2.700 ptas.

Listening Scripts for Quizzes

Quiz 8-1 Capítulo 8 Primer paso

I. Listening

A. LUISA Roberto, ¿qué te gusta para el desayuno?
ROBERTO Me encantan los huevos con tocino. ¿Y a ti?
LUISA A mí me gusta el pan tostado o el pan dulce y para beber, me gusta la leche. Y tú, ¿qué prefieres tomar?
ROBERTO Prefiero el jugo de naranja. También me gustan mucho las frutas, especialmente las toronjas.

Quiz 8-2 Capítulo 8 Segundo paso

I. Listening

A.
1. ¿Qué comes cuando tienes hambre?
2. ¿Qué tomas cuando tienes sed?
3. ¿Cómo está la sopa hoy?
4. ¿Qué hay para el desayuno?
5. La ensalada está deliciosa, ¿no?

Quiz 8-3 Capítulo 8 Tercer paso

I. Listening

A.
1. CLIENTE 1 ¿Cuánto son los batidos?
ROSITA Son mil quinientos sucres cada uno.
2. CLIENTE 2 ¿Y la sopa? ¿Cuánto es?
ROSITA La sopa es seis mil quinientos sucres.
3. CLIENTE 3 Quisiera saber cuánto es el bistec.
ROSITA El bistec cuesta nueve mil cuatrocientos sucres.
4. CLIENTE 4 ¿Y cuánto es la ensalada?
ROSITA ¿La ensalada? A ver. La ensalada es cuatro mil trescientos sucres.
5. CLIENTE 5 Dígame, por favor, ¿cuánto es el pollo?
ROSITA El pollo es ocho mil setecientos cincuenta sucres.

ANSWERS Quiz 8-1

I. Listening

A. (10 points: 2 points per item)

	Luisa	Roberto
1. huevos		✔
2. jugo de naranja		✔
3. leche	✔	
4. pan tostado	✔	
5. tocino		✔

II. Reading

B. (10 points: 2 points per item)

6. almorzamos
7. nos
8. para nada
9. te
10. almuerzo

III. Writing

C. (10 points: 2 points per item)
Answers will vary. Possible answers:

11. Para el desayuno como cereal con leche.
12. Para el almuerzo como un sándwich y papitas.
13. Para el desayuno tomo un vaso de jugo.
14. Para el almuerzo tomo un vaso de leche.
15. Me encanta el tocino.

IV. Culture

D. (5 points: 2 1/2 points per item)

16. b
17. b

ANSWERS Quiz 8-2

I. Listening

A. (10 points: 2 points per item)

1. b
2. c
3. a
4. c
5. a

II. Reading

B. (10 points: 2 points per item)

6. c
7. b
8. a
9. b
10. a

III. Writing

C. (10 points: 2 points per item)
Answers will vary. Possible answers:

11. Buenas tardes. ¿Cómo está la sopa?
12. Está un poco salada y fría.
13. ¿Cómo está la ensalada?
14. Está deliciosa.
15. No me gustaría nada de postre.

ANSWERS Quiz 8-3

I. Listening

A. (10 points: 2 points per item)

1. 1.500
2. 6.500
3. 9.400
4. 4.300
5. 8.750

II. Reading

B. (10 points: 2 points per item)

6. a
7. a
8. b
9. b
10. a

III. Writing

C. (10 points: 2 points per item)
Answers will vary. Possible answers:

11. ¿Me puede traer el arroz con pollo, por favor?
12. Quisiera las zanahorias.
13. No, gracias.
14. Prefiero tomar un refresco.
15. ¿Me puede traer un poco de pan, por favor?

IV. Culture

D. (5 points: 2 1/2 points per item)

16. a
17. b

Scripts for Chapter Test Capítulo 8

I. Listening

A. 1. LUPE Me encanta el arroz con pollo y legumbres.
2. VICTORIA De almuerzo quiero un sándwich de crema de maní y jalea. También quisiera una manzana.
3. HÉCTOR Para mí un perro caliente, papitas y un vaso de té frío.
4. SEBASTIÁN Me gustaría la sopa, un sándwich y un vaso de leche descremada.

B. CARMIÑA Muy bien. Creo que voy a pedir la sopa primero. Luego ¿me trae el arroz con pollo, por favor? Y para beber quisiera un vaso de leche.
CAMARERO ¿Y para usted señor?
MIGUEL Yo quiero un sándwich de jamón y queso. Póngame por favor mostaza, lechuga y tomate.
CAMARERO Muy bien, señor. ¿Y qué desea para tomar?
MIGUEL Para tomar, una taza de café por favor.
CAMARERO ¿Desean postre?
MIGUEL Sí. De postre, quisiera un flan, por favor.
CARMIÑA Para mí, el helado de chocolate.

Answers to Chapter Test

I. Listening Maximum Score: 30 points

A. (8 points: 2 points per item)
1. a
2. c
3. d
4. b

B. (22 points: 2 points per item)
5. a
6. c
7. b
8. c
9. b
10. a
11. a
12. c
13. b
14. c
15. a

II. Reading Maximum Score: 30 points

C. (10 points: 2 points per item)
16. b
17. a
18. a
19. a
20. b

D. (6 points: 2 points per item)
21. c
22. c
23. a

E. (14 points: 2 points per item)
24. hambre
25. almuerzo
26. trae
27. otra
28. Le
29. Me
30. cuenta

III. Culture Maximum Score: 10 points

F. (8 points: 2 points per item)
31. b
32. a
33. b
34. a

IV. Writing Maximum Score: 32 points

G. (12 points: 2 points per item)
Answers will vary. Possible answers:
35. ¿Cómo está la sopa?
36. ¡Ay! No me gusta la sopa para nada.
37. ¿Por qué no le gusta?
38. Está fría y salada.
39. ¿Le puedo traer algo más?
40. No gracias.

H. (10 points)
Answers will vary. Possible answer:
41. Mi comida favorita es el desayuno. Me gusta mucho comer huevos y tocino. Me gusta el tocino porque es muy salado. Me gustan los huevos porque son ricos. Para tomar, me gusta el jugo de naranja porque es muy dulce.

I. (10 points: 2 points per item)
Answers will vary. Possible answers:
42. La cuenta, por favor.
43. ¿Cuánto es?
44. Veintidós mil doscientos cuarenta sucres.
45. ¿Está incluida la propina?
46. Es aparte. La propina es tres mil trescientos sucres.

¡A comer!

DE ANTEMANO

1 Who orders what in the **fotonovela**? Look over the story on pp. 204–205 of your textbook, then match each character with what he or she orders.

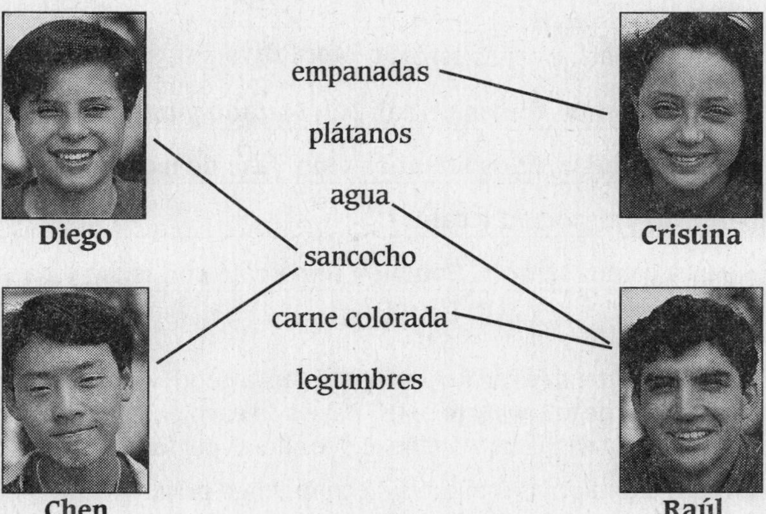

2 Match the different characters' questions on the left with answers on the right. Write the letter of the best response to each question in the blank.

e 1. Raúl, ¿qué es carne colorada?

d 2. Cristina, ¿por qué no vas a pedir el sancocho?

f 3. Diego, ¿no quieres otra empanada?

a 4. Bueno, Chen... ¿qué tal está el sancocho?

c 5. Tengo sed todavía. ¿Vamos a pedir otra botella de agua?

a. Está riquísimo. ¿Quieres un poco?

b. ¡Cuidado! La sopa está muy caliente.

c. ¿Por qué no pides dos? El ají aquí está super-picante.

d. Porque comemos sancocho en casa casi todas las semanas. Hoy quiero empanadas.

e. Es un plato de carne, muy típico del Ecuador... a mí me encanta.

f. No, gracias. Están muy buenas, pero no puedo comer más.

Practice and Activity Book p. 85

PRIMER PASO

3 Breakfast at the Montalvo house is often complicated because each person likes to have something different. Using each drawing, write a sentence asking Luis what each member of the family has for breakfast and then write Luis's answers.

1. 
Raquel y Esteban

2. 
Luis

3. 
Sr. Montalvo

4. 
Sra. Montalvo

1. **Para el desayuno, Raquel y Esteban comen cereal, pan tostado y un vaso de jugo.**
2. **Por lo general, Luis come pan dulce, unos plátanos y un vaso de leche.**
3. **El Sr. Montalvo come huevos con tocino y café.**
4. **A la Sra. Montalvo le gusta comer toronja. También toma café con leche y pan dulce.**

4 Breakfast is the most important meal of the day, but not everyone eats a good breakfast. What nutritional advice do you have for the following people? Based on each person's comments, write one or two sentences telling each one what he or she should eat for breakfast.

MODELO Nunca tomo desayuno. Por las mañanas siempre tengo prisa.
Si siempre tienes prisa, debes comer uno o dos plátanos, pan tostado y un vaso de leche.

1. DIANA Estoy a dieta, y por eso no desayuno nunca.
TÚ **Answers will vary.**

2. CHEMA ¡Uf! No me gusta comer por las mañanas.
TÚ ______________________________

3. EUGENIA Me gustan mucho los huevos y el tocino... pero tienen mucho colesterol.
TÚ ______________________________

4. DIEGO Soy alérgico a *(allergic to)* la leche y el yogurt.
TÚ ______________________________

5. CHUY El médico dice que necesito comer más fruta fresca.
TÚ ______________________________

6. MARÍA ¡Siempre lo mismo! Cereal con leche. Quiero comer algo más interesante de vez en cuando.
TÚ ______________________________

Practice and Activity Book p. 86

5 How do you feel about the following foods? Explain how often you eat them, using **encantar** and **gustar**. Then tell why you like or don't like each one. Is there a food that you really don't like at all? Write about it in number 7.

1. **Answers will vary.**
2.
3.
4.
5.
6.
7. **¡No me gusta(n) ... para nada!**

6 It's late morning and everyone's hungry and thinking about his or her favorite lunch. Write what each of the people in the picture love to have for lunch, using one of the expressions from the box.

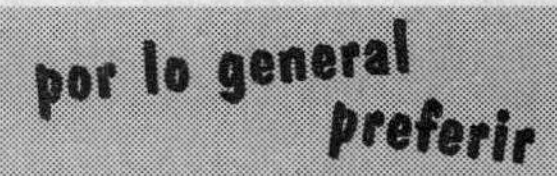

Victoria **Héctor** **Lupe** **Sebastián**

1. **Por lo general, a Victoria le encanta comer un sándwich de crema de maní y una manzana para el almuerzo.**
2. **Héctor prefiere comer un perro caliente, unas papitas y un té frío.**
3. **A Lupe le gusta mucho almorzar arroz con legumbres y pollo y un vaso de limonada.**
4. **Por lo general, Sebastián come sopa de pollo, un sándwich de jamón y un vaso de leche.**

7 A Spanish-speaking magazine is doing a survey to find out more about the eating habits of high-school students. Take part in the survey by completing the questionnaire below.

Cuestionario, 1a parte

1. Cuando estoy enfermo(a), me encanta(n)... ____________
2. Por lo general, no me gusta(n) para nada... ____________
3. Para el desayuno, me encanta tomar... ____________
4. Después del almuerzo, me encanta comer... ____________
5. Antes de dormir me encanta comer... ____________
6. Cuando salgo con mis amigos, nos encanta comer... ____________
7. Los domingos por la mañana me encanta tomar... ____________
8. Por lo general, almuerzo a las... ____________

8 Luisa is babysitting and Sra. Benavides has left a note explaining what each of the Benavides children can and can't eat. Complete her note with forms of the verb **poder** and other words and phrases as needed.

Querida Luisa,

Para el almuerzo, Miguelito 1. **puede** *comer un sándwich de crema de maní. No* 2. **puede** *comer muchas papitas. Susanita y Carlitos* 3. **pueden** *comer la sopa de verduras. Y tú* 4. **puedes** *comer la sopa o comer un sándwich también. De postre todos* 5. **pueden** *comer fruta.*

Para la cena, Susanita no 6. **puede** *comer el pollo porque tiene alergias. Ella* 7. **puede** *comer una hamburguesa. Carlitos y Miguelito* 8. **pueden** *comer el pollo o los espaguetis. De postre, tú* 9. **puedes** *comer helado, si quieres... ¡pero los niños no* 10. **pueden** *comer mucho helado!*

Si tienes un problema, 11. **puedes** *hablar con la vecina, Sra. Aguirre. ¿Y tú, Luisa? ¿Qué* 12. **tomas** *por lo* 13. **general** *para el desayuno? ¿Y qué quieres* 14. **para** *tú almuerzo?*

Buena suerte con todo, y gracias.

Sra. Benavides

Practice and Activity Book p. 88

■ SEGUNDO PASO

9 Everyone has a particular food that he or she can't stand. Read the following cartoon to find out what it is that Juanito hates.

¡Guácala! ¡Qué asco! *Yuck! Gross!*
¿Ya terminaste los coles de Bruselas? *Have you finished your Brussels sprouts?*

How would Juanito answer the question **¿Cómo están los coles de Bruselas?** Circle the number of each sentence below that matches Juanito's reaction to his dinner.

1. "Están deliciosos."
2. (circled) "No me gustan para nada estos coles de Bruselas ."
3. (circled) "¡Estos coles de Bruselas están fríos y salados!"
4. (circled) "¡Uf! No puedo comer estos coles de Bruselas."
5. "Los coles de Bruselas de mi mamá siempre están muy ricos."
6. "Me encanta comer en esta casa."

10 What would you ask or say in the following situations? Using phrases from p. 212 of your textbook and other phrases you know, write two or three sentences to respond to each situation. Be honest, but remember to be polite!

1. You and your friend have swapped lunches today. When you bite into his sandwich, you realize that it's liverwurst and onion.

   Answers will vary.

2. For your mom's birthday, you've made her favorite meal. You want to know what she thinks of the main course and dessert.

   ¿Cómo está el/la...? ¿Y cómo está el postre?

3. As a surprise, your friend invites you to dinner and serves a recipe she just made up on her own: spinach-sardine casserole.

   Answers will vary.

4. The waiter at your favorite restaurant asks how your meal is.

   Answers will vary.

Practice and Activity Book p. 89

5. When you come home from school, someone's been baking and the kitchen is full of chocolate chip cookies.

____

____

11 Look at the **Nota gramatical** on p. 212 of your textbook. Remember that **ser** is used to describe general or typical characteristics of a food. **Estar** is used to describe how particular dishes taste, seem, or look. For each English sentence below, choose the form of **ser** or **estar** to complete the Spanish equivalent.

MODELO These cookies taste great.
Estas galletas (son/están) muy ricas.
Here **están** is the right answer, because the sentence is talking about how these cookies taste, not what cookies in general are like.

1. Soup is good when you're sick.
La sopa (es /está) buena cuando estás enfermo/a.
2. Careful! This pizza is really hot!
¡Cuidado! Esta pizza (es /está) muy caliente.
3. Yuck! The spaghetti is cold.
¡Qué asco! Los espaguetis (son /están) fríos.
4. Mexican food is spicy, right?
La comida mexicana (es /está) picante, ¿verdad?
5. I love chocolate ice cream. It's delicious.
Me encanta el helado de chocolate. (Es /Está) muy rico.
6. Hmm . . . this jelly doesn't taste very sweet.
Mmm... esta jalea no (es /está) muy dulce.
7. Milk is good for children.
La leche (es /está) buena para los niños.

12 In this chapter you've learned how to say more things with the verb **tener**. Do you remember other expressions with **tener** as well? Describe each of the following pictures using at least three expressions with **tener**.

1. Arturo

Answers will vary.

____

____

2. Celia

13 You want to take a survey on eating habits of high school students. Complete this set of questions by asking what students eat or drink

1) when they're hungry or thirsty after class
2) when they're in a hurry
3) when they need a quick lunch

Cuestionario, 2a parte

1. Cuando tengo mucha sed después de clase, me gusta tomar...
2. Cuando tengo mucha **hambre, a veces como...**
3. Por lo general, **cuando tengo prisa me gusta comer...**
4. Mi almuerzo favorito **cuando necesito algo rápido es...**
5. Por la noche, siempre tengo ganas de comer...
6. Si no tengo sueño, por lo general puedo dormir después de comer...
7. Si no tengo mucha hambre para el desayuno, como...

TERCER PASO

14 Find out what seven items you need to set the table by placing the syllables in the correct order. Then write the words out below.

cu so vi ta pla lle ne cha zón cu to ta llo te chi ra ser dor va

Necesito una **cuchara**, un **cuchillo**, un **plato**, una **servilleta**, un **tazón**, un **vaso** y un **tenedor**.

15 Look over the vocabulary for this chapter to complete the crossword puzzle below.

Horizontales

2. La primera comida del día.
6. Una comida que se come *(is eaten)* con jalea en un sándwich.
9. Un marisco *(seafood)* pequeño.
10. Una bebida con mucha vitamina C.
11. Una bebida fría que se hace con limones.
12. Un tipo de legumbre anaranjada.
13. La lista de comidas en un restaurante se llama el ___.
14. La cosa que se usa *(is used)* para limpiar la boca *(mouth)* después de comer.
15. Una legumbre verde y un ingrediente importante en una ensalada.

Verticales

1. Antes de pagar en un restaurante, necesitas pedir la ___.
3. La comida después del desayuno.
4. Una fruta cítrica, más grande que *(bigger than)* una naranja.
5. La comida después del almuerzo.
7. Una agua especial que se sirve *(is served)* en botellas.
8. El atún y el salmón son tipos de ___.
9. La hamburguesa se hace *(is made)* con ___.

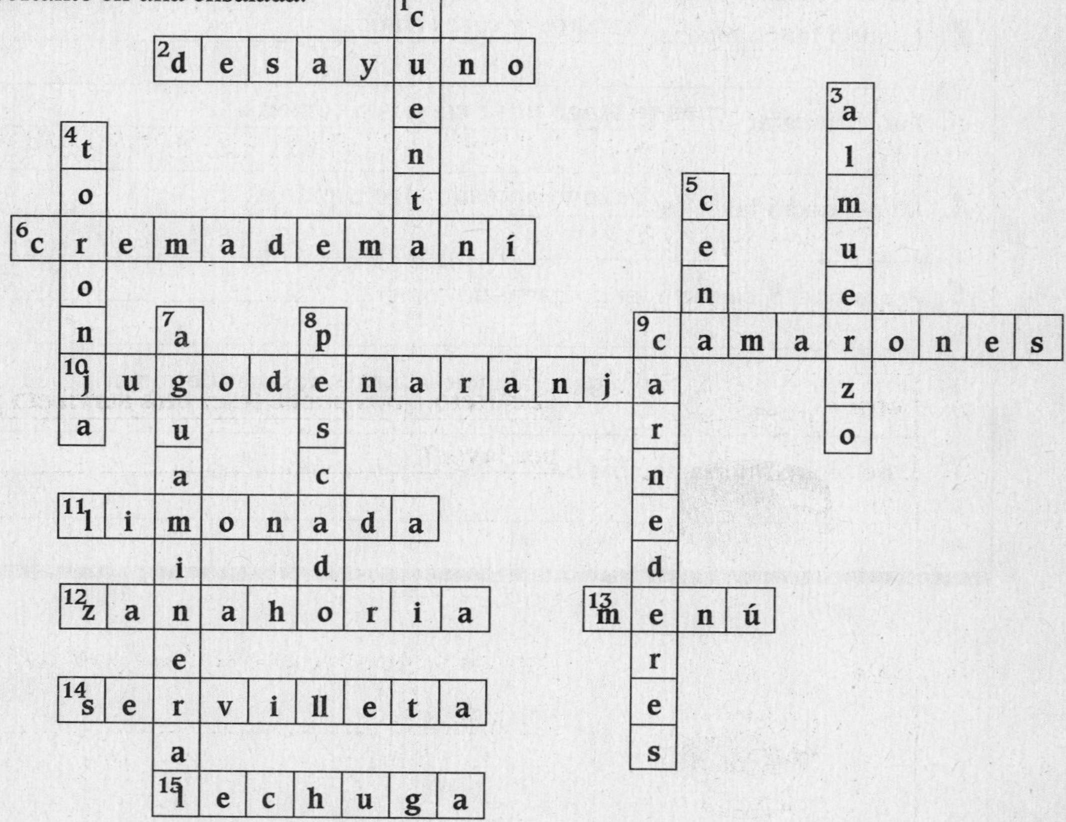

16 You're at the **Café El Rincón** for dinner with a large group of friends. It's your waiter's first day on the job, and he keeps making mistakes with everyone's order. All of the things pictured below are things that he needs to bring you. How would you politely ask for them?

Answers will vary. Possible answers:

1. 

Camarero, ¿nos puede traer tres cuchillos y un bistec por favor?

2. 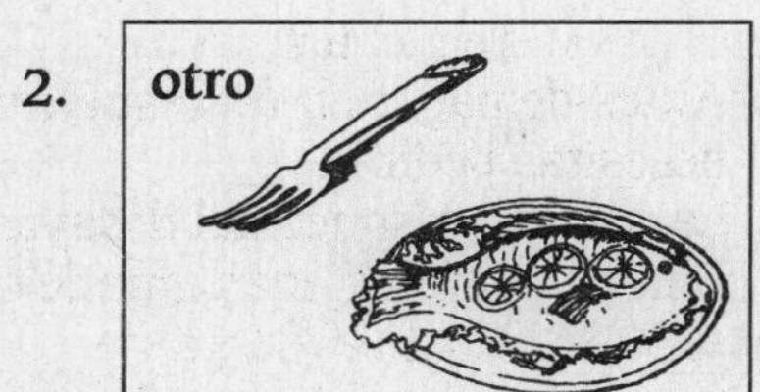

¿Me trae un tenedor y el pescado por favor?

3. 
Camarero, ¿nos puede traer agua mineral y un vaso por favor?

4. 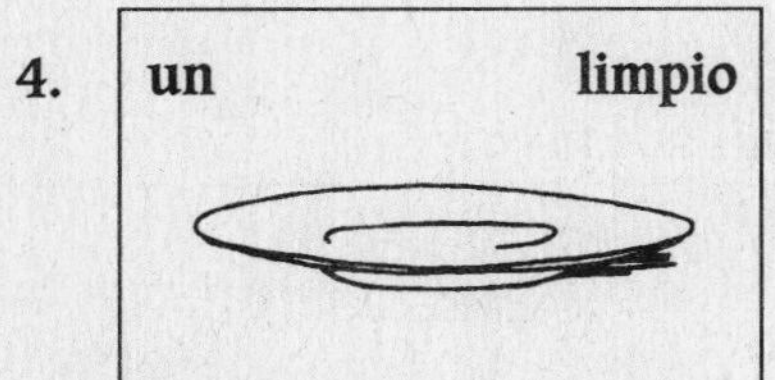

Camarero, ¿me trae un plato limpio? Este plato está sucio.

5. 

Camarero, ¿nos puede traer otra servilleta y el pastel por favor?

6. 

Camarero, ¿me trae otra cuchara y un tazón de helado por favor?

PRACTICE AND ACTIVITY BOOK CAPÍTULO 8 • ANSWERS

Practice and Activity Book p. 93

17 Manuel, Marimar and Sofía are eating out to celebrate Marimar's birthday. Fill in the dialogue according to what takes place in the illustration.

Answers will vary. Possible answers:

SOFÍA Bueno, Marimar, ¿qué **vas a pedir**?

MARIMAR **Voy** a pedir **el pescado con zanahorias y maíz.**

SOFÍA Debes pedir una ensalada también. Ah, aquí viene la camarera.

CAMARERA **Buenas tardes, bienvenidos. ¿Qué les puedo traer?**

SOFÍA ¿Para mí? Bueno, yo **quisiera el arroz con verduras y pollo, por favor.**

MARIMAR A mí **me trae el pescado con zanahorias y maíz**. Ah, y **una ensalada**, también.

CAMARERA Muy bien. Y a usted señor, ¿qué le **puedo** traer?

MANUEL **Para mí, el bistec con papas fritas y una ensalada, por favor.**

CAMARERA Muy bien. ¿Y qué les **gustaría** de tomar?

SOFÍA **¿Nos puede traer tres aguas minerales, por favor?**

CAMARERA ¿Desean algo más? ¿Algún postre?

SOFÍA **Sí, queremos pastel y helado de chocolate, por favor.**

18 You and your friends just finished the meal detailed on this restaurant bill. Create a brief conversation in which the server asks if you want anything else, you answer no and ask for the bill, he or she tells you how much the meal is, and you find out if the tip is included.

El Ranchero
Calle Blanca 44
28012 Madrid
Nº 004169

Cantidad	CONCEPTO	Pesetas
1	Mixta	360
1	Judías verdes	450
1	Salmón	1100
1	Tortilla	300
2	Pan	200
1	Agua	150
1	Kola	150
1	Bombón glacé	300
1	Café	100
	TOTAL	

VAMOS A LEER

19 As you read in the **Nota cultural** on p. 210 of your textbook, lunch (**la comida**) is the main meal of the day in Spanish-speaking countries. It usually consists of a lighter **primer plato** *(first course)* of soup, pasta, vegetables, etc., and is followed by a more substantial **segundo plato** *(main course)* of meat, chicken, or fish. Dessert, often consisting of fresh fruit, is also part of the meal. If this type of lunch seems like a lot of food to you, remember that most Spanish speakers have lighter breakfasts and dinners than we do in the U.S.

Below is a restaurant menu from Spain. As part of the **menú del día** *(daily specials)*, diners choose one **primer plato** and one **segundo plato**, plus **postre** *(dessert)*, in any combination, for a fixed price. Look over the menu, then answer the questions below.

Menú del día 1100 pesetas
Pan, agua o vino y postre incluidos

1er plato
Espaguetis
Ensalada mixta
Sopa de fideos° — *noodles*
Tortilla° de jamón — *omelet*

2ndo plato
Filete de bistec
Bonito° con tomate — *tuna*
Pollo asado° — *roasted*
Gambas al ajillo° — *shrimp in garlic sauce*

Postre
Arroz con leche° — *rice pudding*
Fruta del tiempo
Helados variados

1. Which dishes from the **1er plato** group have pasta? Do any dishes have meat? If so, which ones?

   The spaghetti and the noodle soup; yes the ham omelet

2. What are the seafood dishes in the **2ndo plato** group? If you didn't like seafood, what could you have instead as your second course?

   The shrimp and tuna; you could have roasted chicken or beef

3. What would be a good **1er plato** to eat if it's cold outside? What about if you're on a diet?

   The noodle soup; the salad

4. Look at the choices under **Postre**. What do you think the words **del tiempo** mean when referring to fruit? What does **helados variados** tell you about the assortment of flavors of ice cream this restaurant has?

   In season; there are many different flavors

CULTURA

20 While cereal is the most popular breakfast food in the U.S., it's not as common in Spanish-speaking countries. As you read in the **Nota cultural** on p. 209 of your textbook, breakfast in most Spanish-speaking countries is pretty light. Besides the foods mentioned in your textbook, people will often have **galletas** (crispy, not-too-sweet cookies, sort of like graham crackers) or **magdalenas** (small sweet rolls that taste like pound cake) with breakfast, dunking them in their coffee, chocolate, or milk. If this seems like a skimpy breakfast to you, remember that it's common for people to have a mid-morning **merienda**, or snack, at about 10:00 or 11:00 to tide them over until lunch.

a. Compare breakfast in your house and what you know about breakfast in Spanish-speaking countries. Which style of breakfast do you like better, and why?

Answers will vary.

b. Which seems healthier to you? What are the advantages and disadvantages of each?

21 Look at the **Nota cultural** on p. 214 of your textbook. You may have been surprised to learn that Ecuadorean food is not spicy. In the U.S., a common belief is that food in all Spanish-speaking countries is similar to the spicy dishes of Mexico. Such beliefs about food go both ways. For example, many people in other countries believe that everyone in the U.S. eats fast food all the time.

a. In your opinion, is **la comida norteamericana** really just fast food, or is it something else? Explain.

Answers will vary.

b. Now make a list of five or six breakfast, lunch, dinner, or dessert dishes that you would recommend to a Spanish-speaking tourist who wants to try some "American food."

22 How would you like to go home at midday, eat with your family, and take a short nap or watch TV before going back to classes? While the idea might seem strange to you, it's part of the everyday routine for many students in Spanish-speaking countries, and to them, what you do and eat at lunchtime might seem unusual. Briefly describe your lunchtime routine and compare it to the routine described above. If you could choose, which routine would you rather have?

Answers will vary.

Practice and Activity Book p. 96

VAMOS A LEER

3 A los detalles

1. Les dijo que ellos iban a ser el apoyo de su madre, que tenían que hacerse cargo de la situación y meter el hombro hasta que mandara por ellos.
2. El padre era maestro de primaria. En los Estados Unidos encontró trabajo de ayudante de cocina y de repartidor de periódico.
3. Se sintió completamente feliz de estar junto a su padre y de ver a su familia unida de nuevo.
4. Ha sido muy difícil. El desconocimiento del inglés le ha creado sentimientos de inseguridad muy fuertes.
5. Se refugia pensando en su antiguo país. Idealiza sus recuerdos del mundo en que se sabía aceptado y querido.

4 Vamos a comprenderlo bien

1. *Answers will vary.*
2. *Answers will vary.*
3. *Answers will vary.*
4. *Answers will vary.*
5. *Answers will vary.*

5 Reglas de acentuación: el hiato

1.	a, e, o				
2.	realidad	Mateo	correo	roer	cae
	creas	rodeo	traer	canoa	creer
	feo	trae	Beatriz	sea	leo
3.	re/a/li/dad	Ma/te/o	co/rre/o	ro/er	ca/e
	cre/as	ro/de/o	tra/er	ca/no/a	cre/er
	fe/o	tra/e	Be/a/triz	se/a	le/o

6 Ortografía: las letras *k, qu* y *c*

1. 1. saqué
   2. mascó
   3. busqué
   4. piqué
   5. pescó
2. 1. picó
   2. tocó
   3. pecó
   4. pesqué

VAMOS A ESCRIBIR

7 *Answers will vary.*

VAMOS A CONOCERNOS

8 A escuchar

Students may notice these words: caráota, contiene, típico, época, queso, cocinado, que, poco. *Answers to the second part of this question will vary.*

9 A pensar

Answers will vary.

10 Así lo decimos nosotros

Palabra inglesa	Variante local	Español internacional
I think so	croque sí	creo que sí
fireworks	cuetes	**cohetes**
brain	**celebro**	cerebro
science	**cencia**	ciencia
chance	chanza	**oportunidad**
Christmas	crismas	Navidad
to crack	craquiar	**cuartear/romper**
to shine	chainear	dar brillo/lustre

VAMOS A CONVERSAR

11 *Answers will vary.*